ALIGNING WITH GOD'S APPOINTED TIMES

DISCOVER THE PROPHETIC AND SPIRITUAL MEANING OF THE BIBLICAL HOLIDAYS

ALIGNING WITH GOD'S APPOINTED TIMES

DISCOVER THE PROPHETIC AND SPIRITUAL MEANING OF THE BIBLICAL HOLIDAYS

RABBI JASON SOBEL

FUSION
WITH JASON SOBEL

RJS Publishing

TABLE OF CONTENTS

Jason's Journey

I grew up a nice, Jewish boy from a good, conservative family in New Jersey. I was raised going to Hebrew school but did not want to simply follow the religious rhetoric of my traditional upbringing. I wanted to know this God who the Bible describes as a consuming fire. I had to go on my quest to discover if God was real. I wanted a living, breathing encounter with the uncreated God.

Being Jewish was extremely important to the Sobel household. After all, our family was a living legacy of Holocaust survivors. Most of my mom's relatives died during the Holocaust, so being Jewish was always something deeply ingrained in the very fibers of my being. I grew up with this rich understanding of my identity as a Jew. I had a keen awareness of the need to support the State of Israel, and a love for my Jewish traditions permeated my core identity.

I am not sure if it is humanly possible for a child to enjoy the rigors and religious rituals of Hebrew school. However, I regularly attended Hebrew school as a child. I prepared for my *bar mitzvah* at the age of thirteen and attended synagogue every Saturday morning, learning to read Hebrew and the traditional Jewish prayers. My family wasn't quite *Fiddler on the Roof*, but we were a family of strong moral convictions and traditions. Of course, for me all this was still secondary to baseball and basketball, or the number one priority of hanging out with my friends.

I went looking for new friends in all the wrong places after being unfairly kicked off the school basketball team. I started hanging out with some bad influences. At seventeen years of age, I wound up dropping out of high school, partying with a rough crowd in New York City, and getting in trouble. After staring danger in the face one too many times, I segued out of that life. I was lucky enough to get an engineering internship at a large recording studio in New York City, where many rock and rap stars recorded. I looked at their lives full of fame and fortune, and I saw how unhappy and dysfunctional they and their families were.

I realized I needed something different and something more, and that's when I began my spiritual quest. My best friend, John, introduced me to the martial arts and Eastern philosophy. I began studying and reading Eastern philosophy and religion. Through the process of unanswered questions leading to more questions, I became a "Jew-Bu," a New Age Jew. I was looking for meaning and purpose. I had a hunger and a thirst for the divine and spiritual power in my life. I was willing to travel to the ends of the earth to discover answers to my questions: *Is there a God? For what purpose am I created? Is there more in life than fame and fortune?*

Like a man on a mission, I set my heart on a pilgrimage journey through the unending maze of unanswered questions, which seemed to fill every waking moment. I became very involved with a Jewish New Age teacher who introduced me to an Indian guru named Sai Baba.

Sai Baba is a Hindu legend, who Hindus around the world worship as a god. There is even a Sai Baba land in India. Thousands make an annual pilgrimage to the temple of this

Afro-headed spiritualist, who is said to have transformed flowers into monkeys and heal people and is shrouded in an aura of mysticism and mystery.

When I commit to something, I go all in. So, I gave myself wholeheartedly to the way of Sai Baba. I began sleeping on the floor of my house, became a strict vegetarian, and dreamed of my epic pilgrimage to India to Sai Baba land. It was a small miracle that I did not grow my hair out into a long Afro as well, as imitation is the sincerest form of flattery.

One day while meditating for hours a day and spending large amounts of time studying the teachings of great spiritual masters from India and the East, as well as with my rabbi, I had the spiritual encounter that I had been seeking.

Suddenly, my body began to shake and vibrate violently. I felt a new energy and raw power course through my veins. Perhaps this sounds dramatic to you, but I promise that this experience was authentic. My spirit began to lift out of my body. In this transcendental state, I remember looking down, and I could see my physical body sitting there on the floor, but I felt my spirit floating up and rising higher and higher, and higher.

I went through the roof of my house. I began to fly into the clouds and continue to go up. The next thing I knew, I was in heaven standing before a glorious throne. Seated on this stunning throne, unlike anything I had ever seen, read about, or could scarcely imagine, was Yeshua—Jesus. You may be asking yourself, *How could a nice Jewish boy from Jersey know who Jesus was?* Honestly, there was just something deep inside of me that just knew. To this date, it was the best experience of my life. The encounter was unmatchable in every way and the experience of a lifetime.

My body was vibrating and radiating with energy and power, as well as a deep, abiding undercurrent of complete peace. I was in a state of bliss and euphoria. As I stood before my Maker, moments somehow seemed to slow into eternity. A day can indeed be like a thousand years, and a moment can feel like a lifetime.

Finally, the Lord spoke to me, and I will never forget His words. He said, "Many are called, but few are chosen."

I said, "Lord, am I chosen?"

He sweetly smiled and replied to my question, "Yes."

The next thing I knew, I was no longer in heaven. That euphoric bliss still covered me almost like a light, down blanket, but I was instantly back in my body in my bedroom. I sat in my room again, shrouded with a complete sense of *shalom* (peace) and joy. A peace that surpasses all understanding filled the very marrow of my bones, the cells of my being, and the cavities of my soul. This filling kept me in this state of blissful, perfect peace, and deep contentment. So energized, I ran down the steps into my front yard. I ran around in circles, jumping up and down, screaming at the top of my lungs, "I am called to serve Him! I am called to serve Him!"

Just at this moment, my mom pulled up into the driveway, and she saw her good, little Jewish son running around in circles like a crazy man in her front yard for all the neighbors to gawk at. Surely, she thought I was *mashugana* (a Yiddish term describing a person who is nonsensical, silly, or crazy). I didn't care, as I was so elated, ecstatic, excited, and enamored by the fact that God wanted to use me. Finite words pale in comparison to the reality of the emotions pulsating behind that experience. Although she did not understand what was happening to me, my mother did not want to rain on my parade. There was only one problem. I wondered, *What does it look like for a Jewish man to begin serving Yeshua?* I had no clue. I had no real understanding of Yeshua-Jesus from a biblical perspective since I hardly knew any Christians and had never read the New Testament.

Shortly after my unearthly experience, I was walking out of the front door of a yoga studio in New York City. The shirt I had on said "TRUTH" on the front. A woman coming from the opposite direction approached me.

She said, "Can I ask you a question?"

I said, "Sure."

She asked me, "Do you think the truth is clear, deep, and absolute?"

Her question blew me away because this was exactly what my shirt said ON THE BACK! There was no way she could read what was on the back of my shirt. All of a sudden, she began to *gaze through* me. I became mesmerized and fixated upon her. It was like time began to freeze slowly, and I really couldn't say anything. It was as if we were in a bubble, and all that existed was the two of us. Everything around us began to fade away. She proceeded to tell me how Yeshua-Jesus was the truth, the way, and the life. Energy and power radiated from her that kept me fixed in that spot. I could not move or speak. All I could do was listen to every word that she was saying.

After she spoke to me for what seemed like a long time, the next thing I knew, no one was standing in front of me. It was a crazy spiritual experience. I don't know if she was an angel or what, but I remember thinking to myself, *There's something about this Yeshua, this Jesus. I've encountered Him meditating. Now I've encountered Him through this person on the street.* Something again went off in my mind: I needed to find out who He was, not what New Age teachers or secondary writings in books said about Him. Who did He say He was? Who was this Yeshua whom I encountered face-to-face, and what did He literally teach? What did He want from my life?

By this time, my best friend, John, had become a believer in Yeshua, and he would try to switch me as often as possible.

One day, he called me on the telephone and asked, "You went to Hebrew school as a child, right? Do you think you could tell the difference between the Old and New Testament if I read you some passages?"

I said, "Sure."

He read me the passage of this guy dying on the cross and asked if it was Old or New Testament.

I said, "Obviously, it's the New Testament because it's talking about Jesus."

He read another passage, "He was pierced because of our transgressions, crushed because of our iniquities. . . . Like a lamb led to the slaughter."

He asked, "Is this the Old or New Testament?"

I said, "It must be the New Testament because it sounds like it's talking about Jesus."

John paused, then said, "It's from the Old Testament, from Isaiah, who was a Jewish prophet who lived seven hundred years before Messiah was born" (see Isa. 53:5, 7).

This fact got my attention and began to provoke me to want to learn more.

After our conversation, I agreed to go with him to the messianic synagogue led by Rabbi Jonathan Cahn, who would later write the highly acclaimed and controversial book *The Harbinger*. My friend prayed to lead one Jewish person to faith, but he never thought it would be me. He didn't know it would be possible. The music and message at the synagogue were excellent, and I enjoyed the evening. Then, they dimmed the lights, and Rabbi Jonathan began to lead a prayer for salvation. I figured I needed all the help I could get. I was looking for spiritual enlightenment, so I was more than happy to pray.

It was the first time I had ever prayed to Yeshua-Jesus, and the people said, "Those whose first time it was to pray to Yeshua, please raise your hands."

I raised my hand.

They continued, "If you have raised your hand, please stand up. You've just been born anew."

I had no idea what it meant to be born anew, but I knew it was something a nice Jewish boy should never do. God knows what would happen if I were born again. I gave my mother enough trouble when I was born once. So, I decided not to stand.

Suddenly, a man from Brooklyn said to me, "I saw you raise your hand. If you can't stand here for the Messiah, you won't be able to stand for Him in the world."

I didn't want to make a scene, so I stood up. They brought me to meet with one of the leaders, who began to tell me about the decision I had made. Then, they gave me the first New Testament I had ever seen.

I took it home, not quite sure as to what had just happened. I hid it in my room, and God forbid that my parents should find it. Of course, Mom found it, and she confronted me.

"What is this? Don't tell me you're a Jew who believes in Jesus? You always had to be different. I always knew you'd do something like this one day and break my heart!"

However, I had read the New Testament and believed that Jesus was the one that Moses and the prophets had foretold. He was the one who spoke the words of eternal life. My mom was concerned for me and called our rabbi to meet with me. Knowing I was going to face the rabbi, I knew I had to do further study to verify for myself that Yeshua was the Messiah of the Hebrew Bible. I researched all the messianic promises and prophecies in the Hebrew Scriptures, and I studied in preparation to meet with the rabbi.

The rabbi asked me how I came to believe in Yeshua as Messiah, and I read through all the passages that impacted me. For instance, Daniel 9 talks about when the Messiah was going to come. All the calculations in this chapter point to the time when Yeshua walked the earth. The rabbi researched Daniel and got back to me. He refuted my arguments and said that Daniel was full of metaphors and was an apocalyptic book. He said not to calculate from this book and that he who does brings a curse upon himself. The only bearing the meeting with the rabbi had on me was it gave me a greater hunger and desire to study messianic Judaism.

I found a school that had a messianic Jewish program. I went to summer school there after being a follower of Yeshua for only four months and decided to stay for further studies. During my time there, I realized that Yeshua-Jesus came to make BETTER Jews. All the prophets foretold that the Messiah would bring the Jewish people back to covenantal faithfulness and to strengthen their commitment to Jewish life and their calling to the people of Israel. As a result of my newfound faith, my Jewish identity increased tremendously. Suddenly, everything I had done as a child growing up had profound spiritual significance. I found I had a deeper connection with and understanding of who the Messiah was and what He came to do.

God began to work in new and powerful ways in my life. He said to me, "It's not enough to tell people that God loves them. You need to tangibly show the love, presence, and power of God by praying for people and watch the Kingdom of God break into this age by bringing healing and wholeness into lives." I felt God bringing me back to the power I had experienced initially when I first came to know Him.

One week after coming to faith, I received a phone call from Jeff, a homeless friend in New York City. He had been sleeping on the streets on a cold winter night in Chinatown. His legs had become frostbitten overnight, and he was hospitalized in NYU Medical Center, scared to death that he would not walk again. What did I know? I had read the Gospels and the book of Acts. I thought, "We can do what they did."

John and I went to the hospital to visit him. I had the faith to pray for people and believed that God would make them whole. Jeff was downcast and distraught. His legs were blackish and green. I said, "Jeff, I'm going to pray for you, and I believe that God can heal you." I laid my hands on him and echoed the words of Peter, who said, "Silver and gold I do not have, but what I do have, in the name of Yeshua I say rise, take up your bed and walk" (Acts 3:6, my paraphrase). A couple of days later, Jeff walked out of the hospital on perfect legs.

I knew that this should be not a one-time experience but a normal way of life for followers of Yeshua. I began to step out in faith and pray for healing for people to show the love of God for them. I've seen supernatural manifestations of God's presence and power since that day with Jeff. The apostle Paul says clearly that his teaching doesn't come by wise and persuasive words. It comes with the convincing proof of the Spirit's power so that faith rests not upon the wisdom of men but on the power of God (1 Cor. 2:4).

After this experience with Jeff, I knew I wanted to devote my life to serving God and helping others understand the Jewish roots of their faith. About a year after coming to know Yeshua, I entered into a messianic Jewish studies program and earned a master of arts in intercultural studies with an emphasis on the Hebrew Bible. I also went on to do some study in Israel, which included some time spent studying with traditional rabbis.

In 2005, I was granted rabbinic ordination from UMJC (Union of Messianic Jewish Congregations), resulting in service in many capacities on both a national level and a local level in California.

About Fusion Global

It is in looking back at what God has done that we can see forward to His future plans for us. "'For I know the plans that I have in mind for you,' declares *ADONAI*, 'plans for *shalom* and not calamity—to give you a future and a hope'" (Jer. 29:11). This is what Fusion Global is about.

At Fusion Global with Rabbi Jason Sobel, we want to add definition to your faith as we restore the lost connection to our ancient roots and rediscover our forgotten inheritance.

If we could learn how important Jesus felt these festivals, traditions, and Old Testament teachings were, we would grow to understand how important they should be to us as followers of Yeshua.

By expanding our understanding of prayer and Scripture to include ancient Hebrew and contemporary wisdom informed by the Spirit, we can enrich our perspective of Yeshua (Jesus), His teachings, and His disciples.

PREFACE

Friends, I've written this book to be more than informational. It is an invitation to go on a treasure hunt and discover more of God and His intended blessings for us using the map provided by the celebration of the Jewish holidays. We should never settle for half the inheritance God has willed for us. Let me tell you what I mean by this.

Carefully examine Matthew 13:52. It is a favorite and guiding Scripture passage that drives what I believe: "Therefore every Torah scholar discipled for the kingdom of heaven is like the master of a household who brings out of his treasure both new things and old." I believe the old and new treasures are metaphors Jesus uses for the *Torah*/Old Testament (*roots*) and the New Covenant (*shoots*), as well as Jew and Gentile. All are God's priceless possessions, neither one more or less valuable than the other. However, *together* their value increases dramatically. Who would neglect old treasures just because new treasures exist?

If given an accurate treasure map where X marks the spot, do you think a millionaire or billionaire would turn down the chance to recover lost Spanish bullion from a sunken galleon just because it was five centuries old? Do you think they would say, "Oh, sorry, I have all this new money—really, just keep the old treasure"? It's a ridiculous thought and an unnecessary compromise! Treasure is treasure—old or new.

A biblical story that tells the tragedy of unnecessary compromise is the account of Esau and Jacob. Genesis 25:29–34 discloses how Esau came home famished from the fields one day. He begged for a bowl of red pottage from his twin brother, Jacob, who was a schemer and an opportunist. Esau was so incredibly hungry that he sold his birthright as the firstborn to Jacob in return for a bowl of stew. This compromise is an outrageous trade-off. In Jewish tradition and biblical law, the firstborn male had a unique status concerning inheritance rights and other regulations. Trading this special privilege away is the same nonsensical logic as settling for just old or new treasure. Like Esau, we absurdly compromise our full inheritance if we settle for less than the whole.

In Galatians 3:28, Paul states, "There is neither Jew nor Greek [Gentile] . . . for you are all one in Messiah *Yeshua.*" The revelation of our **unity** in Yeshua (Jesus' Hebrew name) has produced a hunger in me for this **full** inheritance, this abundant blessing, offered by God. We don't have to compromise. We have a treasure map that points to all the treasure and inheritance we have in Yeshua.

How about you? Are you ready to take advantage of your full inheritance?

The biblical Jewish holidays are part of the inheritance of ALL followers of the Messiah. The holidays, steeped in tradition and rich in profound meaning, can become a common ground unifying Jews and Gentiles, which is my goal for this book. Once Gentiles understand these sacred times of the year, they will experience or "see" their faith in *high-definition.*

Here's an example from my life. A while back, I succumbed to temptation and bought a hi-def TV. I couldn't wait to watch the Super Bowl in HD. But I was disappointed by the picture quality, which was very different than what I saw on the model TV in the store. Was HD just a bunch of hype, I wondered? Toward the end of the game, I started flipping through the channels. All of a sudden, I had a revelation! I discovered that the higher channels were the HD ones. I moaned to myself as I realized with disappointment that I hadn't watched the game on the hi-def station. I could not believe the difference and the richness of the picture. The color! The detail! It was like watching a different game.

One of the key points in this funny story is that I had not realized my loss—not watching the game in HD—until I changed channels and had a comparison.

Similarly, by understanding and celebrating the Jewish holidays, we introduce ourselves to the Jewish roots of our faith and gain a heightened perspective. We practice the same traditions and rituals that Yeshua-Jesus embraced. We begin to see His life and ministry from a different viewpoint, through Jewish eyes. It's like high-definition television compared to a black-and-white or low-definition model. When you see in HD, there is greater richness, sharpness, and clarity of details that you would have missed without it. There is a greater revelation of what exists on the screen. Like my Super Bowl experience, before I changed channels, I had no idea what I was missing. I enjoyed the game, but when I flipped to the hi-def station, I appreciated the fullness of the picture from a different, enhanced perspective.

The Jewish holidays give us a means to experience God in HD. They give us a way to connect to the Jewish foundations of our faith and allow us to tap into their rich wells of revelation and wisdom.

Another crucial reason encouraging us to study the Jewish holidays is that when the Jewish *roots* and Gentile *shoots* connect, spiritual revelation, renewal, and transformation occur. I believe a notable example of this is found in Luke 24 as two disciples were on the road to Emmaus after the death of Yeshua. These two grieving men were on their way to a town when a man encountered them. The man was Yeshua-Jesus, but they didn't recognize Him. He questioned their sadness, and they recounted the horror and disappointment of the previous days.

> *Yeshua* said to them, "O foolish ones, so slow of heart to put your trust in all that the prophets spoke! Was it not necessary for Messiah to suffer these things and to enter into His glory?" Then beginning with Moses and all the Prophets, He explained to them the things written about Himself in all the Scriptures. They approached the village where they were going, and He acted as though He were going farther on. But they urged Him, saying, "Stay with us, for it is nearly evening and the day is already gone." So He went in to stay with them. And it happened that when He was reclining at the table with them, He took the *matzah*, offered a *bracha* [blessing] and, breaking it, gave it to them. Then their eyes were opened and they recognized Him, and He disappeared from them. They said to one another, "Didn't our heart burn within us while He was speaking with us on the road, while He was explaining the Scriptures to us?" (Luke 24:25–32)

Jesus showed them that all their experiences with Him were linked to what Moses and the prophets prophesied thousands of years before. Yeshua-Jesus did a spiritual version of connect-the-dots, linking together how He fulfilled all the Old Testament prophecies. He joined the old to the new, the *roots* to the *shoots*. It was then that the lights went on and the disciples tuned in to the right channel. They discovered the big picture (in HD).

When we see how the *shoots*/New Covenant join with the *roots*/*Torah*, it is a revelation that causes our hearts to burn within us just as the disciples of long ago. A fiery yearning for Yeshua, a passion for the *Torah*, and a desire for the *Brit Hadasha*, the New Covenant, combine to ignite a fire that renews and transforms us. It becomes our *personal* road to Emmaus experience.

One night, after a Bible study, a man came up to me and asked, "How could all the details fit together so perfectly thousands of years apart? Statistically, it is too amazing to be by mere chance. Even if I didn't believe in Yeshua, and I heard this, I would come to believe, based on the fact that there is no way anyone could ever put all these things together."

The sacrifice of the ultimate Gardener grafted Gentile followers of Yeshua into the Jewish olive tree. These followers are the branches. But what gives life to the branches? The roots provide sustenance and nourishment, vitality, and growth. For the followers of the Messiah to keep growing in vitality, renewal, and revelation, we must reattach to the roots and remain attached. For what happens to a branch cut off from the tree? It remains alive, looking the same, for only a short time until the lack of nourishment causes it to wither and die before its time.

Understanding and celebrating the Jewish holidays are essential ways Gentile followers can restore themselves to the Jewish roots of the faith and stay connected. Remember, Jesus said in John 15:4, "Abide in Me, and I will abide in you. The branch cannot itself produce fruit, unless it abides on the vine. Likewise, you cannot produce fruit unless you abide in Me." I believe embracing the feasts that He embraced is one of the ways to abide in Him.

Moreover, acknowledging the appointed feasts is a key means by which Gentiles can reconcile themselves to the Jewish people. There was never meant to be a separation. This is what Paul writes in Ephesians 2:11–12:

> Therefore, keep in mind that once you—Gentiles in the flesh . . . were separate from Messiah, excluded from the commonwealth of Israel and strangers to the covenants of promise, having no hope and without God in the world. But now in Messiah *Yeshua*, you who once were far off have been brought near by the blood of the Messiah.

I genuinely believe most Gentiles do not know this following truth. Yet it is one of the most driving factors that led me to write this book: **Israel must be saved for Jesus to return; the redemption of the Jewish people hastens the return of the**

Messiah! Jesus, Himself, plainly states that He will not return until Israel says, "*Baruch ha-ba b'shem Adonai.* Blessed is He who comes in the name of the LORD!" (Matt. 23:39). Outreach to Israel and the Jewish people accelerates the redemption of the nations. Observing the feasts builds a bridge and creates a common bond between Jew and Gentile, which can lead to relationships and make the Messiah known to His people. It is only through these connections that people's hearts can change by the transforming love of the Messiah. Jesus ate with people, walked and talked with people, visited them in their homes—He invested Himself in them. There's a saying: "People don't care what you know until they know that you care." Yeshua-Jesus cared.

We are called to care as well. Yeshua-Jesus commissions us in Matthew 28 to "go therefore and make disciples of all nations" (v. 19). This verse is widely known as the Great Commission. Sadly, somewhere along the way, we dropped the C, creating the Great Omission, which is the failure to share the love of the Messiah with the Jewish people from whom and to whom He came. I believe the enemy has blinded the Gentile church to know how truly Jewish their Messiah is. As we said, the nations at Yeshua-Jesus' time were to become partakers of the promises of God. However, what has happened over time is that we have become over-takers of those promises. There has been false teaching, known as "replacement theology," that the church has replaced the Jewish people. This is untrue.

In Romans, Paul writes, "I am not ashamed of the Good News, for it is the power of God for salvation to everyone who trusts—to the Jew first and also to the Greek [Gentile]" (1:16). If we are going to share the message, we need to share it with the Jew first because that is where it came from. Paul was a Jew. Yeshua was Jewish. They brought the message and hope of redemption to the kingdoms and nations. Now, it is the responsibility of the nations to make sure the message gets back to the Jewish people. Paul writes in Romans 11:25–27:

> A partial hardening has come upon Israel until the fullness of the Gentiles has come in; and in this way, all Israel will be saved, as it is written, "The Deliverer shall come out of Zion. He shall turn away ungodliness from Jacob. And this is My covenant with them, when I take away their sins."

Many of the first-century Jews did not recognize the Messiah, but there was a remnant who did, and they brought Him to the world. We understand from the verse above that a day is coming when the fullness of the Gentiles will come in, and the fullness of redemption will come again to the Jewish people. Look at what Romans 11:12 has to say: "Now if their [the Jews'] transgression leads to riches for the world, and their loss riches for the Gentiles, then how much more their fullness!" Verse 16 goes on to say, "If the root is holy, so are the branches."

Lastly, but certainly by no means least, another compelling reason to recognize the Jewish holidays is Jesus—the Messiah Himself—celebrated the Jewish festivals. More importantly, every major event in Yeshua's life occurred on the *chagim*, on one of the Jewish holidays. For instance, Yeshua-Jesus was in all likelihood born around the time of *Sukkot*, the festival that focuses on God's presence, provision, and protection. Jesus' death was on Passover, the holiday that promises redemption. Did you know that the Last Supper of our Lord was a Passover *seder*?

Can you start to see how understanding the holidays give us a deeper understanding and greater insight into the person and work of Yeshua? Since much of Jesus' life and ministry as recorded in the Gospels revolve around the festivals, a *full* revelation of Yeshua is ours when we grasp these appointed times.

On the lighter side, you will find that our God is not merely about fasting but also about feasting. He is a God of celebration. He wants you to come and join His party. So, let's celebrate as Jesus did.

And the LORD spoke to Moses, saying, "Speak to the children of Israel, and say to them: 'The feasts of the LORD, which you shall proclaim to be holy convocations, these are My feasts. Six days shall work be done, but the seventh day is a Sabbath of solemn rest, a holy convocation. You shall do no work on it; it is the Sabbath of the LORD in all your dwellings. These are the feasts of the LORD, holy convocations which you shall proclaim at their appointed times.'"
Leviticus 23:1–4 NKJV

INTRODUCTION

The Lord said to Moses, "Speak to the Israelites and say to them: 'These are my appointed festivals, the appointed festivals of the Lord, which you are to proclaim as sacred assemblies.'"
Leviticus 23:1–2 NIV

GOD'S DIVINE APPOINTMENTS WITH MAN

When your husband or wife, boyfriend or girlfriend tells you they want to set aside time to spend with you, do you pencil them in? I can tell you many wives I know wouldn't respond too kindly to that reply. Many couples find time away from the demands of life to be with and focus on one another. Let's face it: In the mounting busyness of daily living, the quality of our relationships is defined by the amount of time we spend on them, right?

Now, what if the Creator of the universe asked you to set aside time for Him? That is the question God is asking in the Leviticus 23 passage quoted above. He knew that our world would become increasingly hectic; paradoxically, time would shrink to short supply as we tooled technology to do more for us. God considers us so significant that He preappointed times to meet with us. Though it may sound archaic in a digital age, God didn't just pencil Himself in but penned in appointments that weren't to be changed by life. These sacred assemblies are to be permanently programmed in our calendars, shifting and ordering our lives around them. What a concept!

In both Matthew 6:33 and Luke 12:31, Jesus tells us to seek the Kingdom of God above all else. I believe observing the feasts is one of the ways about which He was speaking. You will see in the chapters that follow that when we order our lives around the sacred assemblies, this order brings incredible spiritual insights. We begin to live with a purpose that focuses on what God has done historically, what He is doing now, and what He plans to do in the future. This spiritual purpose shapes and transforms our lives.

IN THE BEGINNING

In the beginning God created the heavens and the earth.
. . . Then God said, "Let lights in the expanse of the sky be
for separating the day from the night. They will be for signs
and for seasons [mo'adim] and for days and years."
Genesis 1:1, 14

Why did God create the sun, moon, and stars? They are not merely ornaments strung in the sky for decoration or only instruments for telling time or navigation; instead, *creation* points to the *Creator*. The sun, moon, and stars usher God's people into worship and a sense of awe and wonder about Him. Deeply woven into the very fabric of creation is worship.

All of creation also points us to the Jewish celebrations. Why do I say this?

The Hebrew word *mo'adim* means "appointed times" or "festivals" and is used in the Genesis quote above in the same way it appears in Leviticus 23, which describes seven biblical holidays termed "appointed festivals [*mo'adim*]." The heavenly bodies such as the sun and the moon ("lights in the expanse of the sky") are for appointed times (i.e. "seasons" [*moadim*]). From Leviticus 23, we understand that the appointed times are not the seasons of the year—fall, winter, spring, summer—but the times of worship set forth by God as the festivals.

What are these divine dates?

They are the Jewish holidays—**Passover, Pentecost, *Purim, Chanukah, Yom Kippur***, and so on. They are meant for us to be with and focus on the One who created us. They are our opportunity to step away from life as usual and connect with the Source of life, to gain nourishment from and nurture our relationship with Him.

Our life is to be ordered around these appointments, these *God-togethers*, and NOT shifted based on our availability. To me, it's beautiful—something permanent and steadfast in a world that prides itself on the shifting sands of "new and improved." Don't get me wrong. I love progress, but there is something to be said about having deep roots in tradition. A beautiful balance between the two bears the best fruit—forward motion informed and molded by history. The Jewish holidays, or feasts, not only help us to remember and celebrate what God has done in the past, but they *prophetically* reflect what He will do in the future.

LOOK BACK TO SEE FORWARD

The word *prophetic* may be unfamiliar to you. In the context of exploring the Jewish holidays for this book, *prophetic* means "future fulfillment of biblical promises concerning the Messiah and the redemption of the world." What is *to come* is revealed by what God *has already done*. The Jewish holidays are more than sacred assemblies. They are divine mirrors, reflecting God's intentions for the future by what He has done in the past. This kind of divine reflection may be a new concept to you, but I will clarify. Once you grasp this truth, you will embrace it as precious, as understanding the feasts puts your finger on the pulse of the Father, revealing His heart. God doesn't seek to be a mystery; rather, He wants to be a divine DISCOVERY! He desires to make Himself known.

Let's take an overview of the holidays and the specific focus, or *promise*, of each one. Are you ready for the journey that will take you deeper into the heart of God?

OVERVIEW: THE FEASTS AND THE FOCUSES

THE PROMISE OF EACH SEASON	
Shabbat:	*Rest, remembrance, and restoration*
Passover:	*Redemption*
Firstfruits:	*Resurrection*
Pentecost:	*Revelation and gift of the Word and the Spirit*
Rosh Hashanah:	*Repentance, restoration, and returning/regathering to God*
Yom Kippur:	*Reparation and redemption/forgiveness from sin (fullness of redemption)*
Sukkot:	*Rejoicing and thanksgiving for God's presence, protection, and provision, as well as the establishment of God's Kingdom*
Chanukah:	*Rededicating ourselves to God*
Purim:	*Rejoicing and realizing that God is in control even though His hand is hidden*

Leviticus 23 clearly defines this divine appointment calendar and breaks it up into three cycles. The weekly celebration of *Shabbat* is the first holiday mentioned. This word means "to rest" in Hebrew. It marks the weekly Sabbath, starting at sundown on Friday and ending at sundown on Saturday. God rested on the seventh day, so we do as He did. Rest from work is mandatory, allowing time to gather with family and recount your blessings. This rest also enables us to remember Him as Creator and Redeemer and thank Him for this life as well as eternal life. *Shabbat* can be looked upon as a weekly Passover in that we remember our redemption. Through redemption comes restoration of our relationship to God and our fellow man. We are restored to the garden.

The spring holidays are **Passover**, **Firstfruits**, and **Pentecost**. These are holidays that reflect God's work of the past. The *first* coming of the Messiah **fulfilled** them. If you're scratching your head, let me explain in brief here and in-depth later on in the book.

The focus of **Passover** (*Pesach* in Hebrew) is *redemption*, which leads to freedom. The Lord redeemed the Israelites from Egypt, freeing them from the bondage of slavery. Centuries later, Jesus (*Yeshua* in Hebrew) died as the Passover Lamb to redeem us from death and break the bondage of sin. Redemption in the days of Moses was meant to mirror redemption through the death of the Messiah. Yeshua-Jesus is the ultimate fulfillment of the promise of redemption.

During the celebration of **Firstfruits** (*Yom HaBikkurim*), the focus is *resurrection*. Firstfruits was an agricultural holiday that celebrated the firstfruits of the harvest, which were brought from the fields to the temple. Fittingly, thousands of years later, Jesus was brought back from the dead during this festival.

In 1 Corinthians 15:20, Paul tells us, "But now Messiah is risen from the dead, the firstfruits of those who have fallen asleep." Though Jesus fulfilled the promise of this holiday in His resurrection, there is also a *prophetic* fulfillment as firstfruits of the harvest symbolize the future coming harvest of believers at the end of the age.

Pentecost (*Shavuot*) focuses on *revelation*. This holiday commemorates the giving of the *Torah* to Moses on Mount Sinai. During Jesus' time on earth, He gave the gift of the Holy Spirit to the disciples in Jerusalem on Pentecost. There is something significant about the fact that God chose the same day, both in the Old Testament and New Testament, to give the gift of Word and Spirit. Word and Spirit combine to bring us greater revelation. In Genesis 1, the Spirit hovered over the formless face of the watery earth, and then God spoke the words "Let there be light." And there was light. Word and Spirit couple to bring about new creation and greater revelation.

Redemption, resurrection, and revelation—Jesus fulfilled the focus or *promise* of all three spring holidays during His lifetime.

The fall holidays are **Rosh Hashanah, Yom Kippur,** and **Sukkot.** These are awaiting their prophetic or *future* fulfillment.

Rosh Hashanah (Feast of Trumpets) is the Jewish New Year and is "trumpeted in" with the blowing of the *shofar*. This holiday points to *repentance* (changing one's way of thinking and being), *resolving* to make a better life, and ideally *returning* or *re-gathering* to God. At the sound of the *shofar* in a day yet to come, God will gather all His people from the four corners of the earth to Himself at the return of the Messiah (Matt. 24:31).

Yom Kippur means "atonement," or to *repair* a wrong so that we can be one with the Holy One. (Notice, we can separate the word *atonement to at-one-ment*). This feast also focuses on *repentance and redemption/forgiveness* from the sins of the previous year. In the future fulfillment of this holiday, all Israel, as well as the nations, will look upon the One whom they pierced and recognize Him as the Messiah. Looking upon Yeshua will result in the realization of the fullness of *redemption*. In Jewish thought, it is the final redemption.

Sukkot (Feast of Shelters) is a time for *rejoicing*. This holiday commemorates the wandering of the Israelites in the desert. The shelters relate to the temporary structures in which they lived as they wandered. It remembers how God provided *manna* from heaven to feed them, water from the stones to quench them, and a pillar of cloud by day and fire by night to guide them. Ultimately, it reflects God's presence, provision, and protection. Appropriately, some scholars believe that Jesus was born during this holiday. With the fulfilling of the future promise of *Sukkot*, the Kingdom of God will be established, and we will all rejoice.

In addition to the fall and spring holidays, which are known as the major holidays and found in Leviticus 23, there are two other minor, but crucial, holidays mentioned in Scripture—*Purim* and *Chanukah*.

Purim is found in the book of Esther. Intrigue, sabotage, fear, courage, romance and rising to one's destiny—it may sound like a soap opera, but it is another chronicled struggle between good and evil where the hidden hand of God isn't seen but is at work on behalf of the people who belong to Him. The story of Esther and the celebration of *Purim* are ultimately about God working all things together for the good of those who love Him (Rom. 8:28).

We *realize* that when we cannot see the providential hand of God, we must trust the heart of God. Realizing the goodness of the Father stirs us to *rejoice*!

Chanukah is the Feast of Dedication found in both the book of Daniel and the Gospel of John. It commemorates the miraculous *rededication* of the temple in Jerusalem after the Greeks defiled it in the second century BC. This feast honors and celebrates the miracles God did, such as one night's cruise of oil for the menorah providing for eight nights' worth of light and the victory of the outnumbered Israelites over the imperious Greeks. God delivered the many into the hands of the few, proving Zechariah 4:6: "'Not by might, nor by power, but by My *Ruach* [power]!' says *Adonai-Tzva'ot* [the LORD of Hosts]." Many scholars and Bible teachers believe that Jesus called Himself "the light of the world" in John 8 and 9 during *Chanukah*. This holiday's prophetic fulfillment is when the light of the Messiah shines forth to all the ends of the world and we become the light that God calls us to be.

It is in looking back at what God has done that we can see forward to His future plans for us. "'For I know the plans I have in mind for you,' declares *ADONAI*, 'plans for *shalom* and not calamity—to give you a future and a hope'" (Jer. 29:11).

THE GIFT THAT KEEPS GIVING

The *Present* Present

Another way to look at the Jewish holidays is not only as divine mirrors reflecting historical events and future promises but also as gifts that keep giving in the *present*. Let me explain.

There are two Hebrew words for the biblical holidays. The first is the word *moedim*, which is used in Leviticus 23 and is best translated as "appointed times." A *moed*, the singular form of *moedim*, means an "appointed festival" or an "appointed place," as in the *Ohel Moed*, the "Tent of Meeting." The *Ohel Moed*/Tent of Meeting is the place where God spoke with and met with Moses: "Now *ADONAI* called to Moses and spoke to him out of the Tent of Meeting [*Moed*]" (Lev. 1:1). What is the connection between these two uses of the word *moed*? The biblical holidays are spiritually meant to be like a "tent in time" in which we can enter and encounter God in unique ways. In other words, God has appointed times in which we can connect with Him and tap into the spiritual meaning of that designated *moed*/holiday.

The second Hebrew word is *chag*, which means "holiday" or "circle." The Jewish holidays are days of remembrance. We remember what God did for our ancestors on these days and at those times. But the *chagim*, holidays in the plural, are more than just mere remembrances; they are meant to be recurrences. They are reactivations of past occurrences—meaning that what happened in the past at this time and season can recur repeatedly in our own lives and communities.

Past historical events that were carried out by God don't just pass away but remain living and active. They are always present in some sense. The Hebraic view of time and history is not static but dynamic; thus, the biblical holidays are past historical events that continue on a spiritual level to be active in the present. So, by tapping into what the Lord did in the past, we can relive and experience it in the present. For example, at Passover God wants to remind us that He is the Redeemer, and He desires for us to experience true freedom from any kind of physical, emotional, or spiritual bondage HERE and NOW. We can celebrate and relive what He did in the past today.

The holidays are NOT just to remember what He has done in the past or to look forward to what He will do in the future. He wants us to keep experiencing the focus and promise of each holiday in increasingly more significant measures every day/year, on deeper levels, and in more transformative ways. These appointed times are God's gifts that keep on giving!

The biblical holidays are clearly days of destiny and times of transformation.

DIVINE DRAMA
The Physical Experience of the Holidays

Please don't misunderstand me; I'm not talking daytime soaps or nighttime sagas. The appointed feasts are an eternal, divine drama. They tell the story from creation, celebrated during *Rosh Hashanah*, believed to be the birthday of creation in Jewish thought, to the establishment of the Kingdom of God, celebrated during *Sukkot*. The Jewish people don't just celebrate the holidays; we become participants in the story. Shakespeare called the world a stage. God designed His appointed festivals as a stage for His story. Like any good actor, we don't just recite the lines but experience the part.

What do I mean by this?

The Jews don't just cognitively tell the story of any of the feasts; we do specific things at specific times, engaging our different senses. This holistic approach to the holidays allows us not only to learn but experience and subsequently be transformed by them. It is also a very effective way to disciple present and future generations.

An example of this sensory engagement is during the *seder* meal at Passover. We recite blessings and prayers at certain times, then eat of bitter herbs dipped in saltwater representing the tears of our enslaved ancestors. There are also dishes prepared with horseradish to symbolize the bitterness of bondage. I can tell you that these dishes can set off a five-alarm fire in your mouth! All your senses engage as you grab for the grape juice to stop the sting. When I was growing up, my household referred to it as Jewish Dristan—it will definitely clear your sinuses!

At a certain point in the meal, we drink from four cups of wine that represent our freedom and allow us to taste the sweetness of it. Do you see what I'm saying?

In some ways, the feasts are meant to bring a *tikkun*, a correction for the Fall of man where all our senses were involved, except for smell, and came out of alignment with heaven. By engaging our senses to serve God during the holidays, we sanctify them and realign them.

JESUS' FINAL PRAYER REQUEST

In the Preface, I wrote about how celebrating the feasts gives us better insight into Jesus because these were the holidays He celebrated. I want to offer you another revelation into our Lord.

An expression that belongs to yesteryear is "From your mouth to God's ears." Have you heard that before? Let me turn it around for the next point I want to make: "From *God's* mouth to *our* ears."

Do you know what Jesus prayed for in His final prayer in John 17? "Holy Father, keep them in Your name that You have given Me, so that they may be one just as We are" (v. 11). The Messiah's final prayer discloses His heart toward **unity**. God's presence, power, and provision are closely linked to the unity of His people. The unification of the *roots* and the *shoots*—the old and the new treasures, the Jews and the Gentiles—was so important to Jesus that it was His final prayer request in the last hours of His life. Imagine—it is within **our** power to answer the Messiah's prayer. *From His lips to our hearts!*

Hebrews 13:8 assures us, "*Yeshua* the Messiah is the same **yesterday, today, and forever**." Be prepared to be introduced anew to an unchanging Abba/Father and Savior/Son. This journey into the Jewish appointed times will lead you into profoundly new encounters with the Creator. This encounter becomes possible from a profound revelation and awakening that ushers you into new levels of awareness. In other words, you and your faith can't remain the same.

SUMMARIZING THE SACRED

In closing, remembering the sacred assemblies is important for these reasons:

- The holidays are God's permanently penned appointments with us.

- Jesus Himself embraced and celebrated the holidays. We gain a greater understanding of Him when we understand the feasts.

- Celebrating the feasts restores the Gentile *shoots* to the Jewish *roots* and foundations of our faith, allowing us to experience God with greater insight and revelation (in HD).

- The holidays are a bridge over the fissure caused by the fragmentation between Jews and Gentiles. Observing the festivals will help to close the chasm and unify God's people, which is His heart for us.

- Recognizing these appointed times creates a common ground between Gentiles and Jews, extending the love of the Messiah to His people. The sooner the Jews come to the Messiah, the sooner the Messiah comes.

Shabbat is an oasis in the midst of the desert of time that refreshes and rejuvenates our body and soul. God Himself rested on the *Shabbat*, not because He was tired but because He wanted to model for us its great importance.

CHAPTER ONE

Shabbat

THE SABBATH REST OF HEAVEN

Work may be done for six days, but the seventh day is a Shabbat of solemn rest, a holy convocation. You are to do no work—it is a Shabbat to ADONAI in all your dwellings.

Leviticus 23:3

THE FIRST DATE

Shabbat is the first holiday God penned/programmed in our appointment calendar with Him. The focus of this holiday is to *rest, remember,* and *restore.* It is probably the most significant holiday, as it occurs weekly. It is the seventh day, the Sabbath. It is also the most countercultural of the holidays—but in a right way. You will see what I mean when we look at

The Promise of Rest . . .

Shabbat in Hebrew means "to rest," "to cease," "to put an end to," "to stop completely." This concept of rest is an insult to the pace of today. Most of us think of the Sabbath as two hours on one day of the week. I call this "Fast-Food Spirituality," which is in keeping with our microwave mentality—done in thirty seconds.

God works on a different clock. He usually is in no hurry. The biblical Sabbath is twenty-five hours, from sundown on Friday to one hour after sundown on Saturday. Leviticus 23 instructs us to stop all work and gather together for "solemn assembly." This assembly is more than physically gathering within congregational walls. *Shabbat* is a gathering of ourselves emotionally and spiritually to rest and turn our attention and energy to God, family, and friends.

SHABBAT SHALOM

Shabbat Shalom is the common Hebrew greeting for the Sabbath. *Shalom* can mean peace, which often connotes the absence of conflict. However, the word represents more than peace. *Shalom* is physical, emotional, and relational *wholeness.* It is a holistic wholeness. Nothing broken, nothing missing. It is an inner peace **above** circumstance. It is the peace Yeshua-Jesus talks about in John 14:27: "*Shalom* I leave you, **My *shalom* I give to you**; but not as the world gives!" *Shalom* is transcendent.

ENTER THE REST

There remains a Shabbat *rest for the people of God. For the one who has entered God's rest has also ceased from his own work, just as God did from His. Let us, therefore, make every effort to enter that rest.*
Hebrews 4:9–11

The quote above reminds us that God rested. The writer of Hebrews ends this statement with a warning that if we don't enter this rest, "we will fall." Many of us HAVE fallen. We pop peace in the form of pills. Relationships are in shreds, evidenced by divorce rates (within the church and without) reaching 50 percent of marriages. We ask ourselves, *Why?* The answer isn't apparent, and its illusiveness is lethal.

Time, or the lack thereof, is the reason for our fall. We can't rest if we don't take the time. We can't grow or nurture relationships if we don't take the time. Anything worthwhile requires it. No substitutions.

Think in practical, physical metaphors. Good food takes time to prepare. You're not going to microwave a gourmet meal, are you? Will you ask the surgeon to rush and get the transplant done in an hour? The work of our careers takes a significant investment of time. If we breeze through a demanding project, the outcome will most likely fall short of expectations, and we suffer the consequences by losing the job, the client, and so on.

If we make time for the physical and material things of this world, which are temporal, why would we or do we shortchange the eternal? The saying "We can't take it with us" applies. The Egyptians thought they could, but it didn't work out so well, as many tomb robbers will concur. I have never personally seen a U-Haul truck following a hearse.

Spirituality needs time as well. You can't go deep with God on the go. It just doesn't work, and this is what I mean by *Shabbat* being countercultural. It demands time—twenty-five hours to be exact—and this is a TALL order for our culture.

God had to bring forth time and space in which to create.

Observing *Shabbat* is about mastering time to rest and to have a relationship with God and others. But resting is more than ceasing work. You can be physically still but in nervous knots internally. Your mind can still be buzzing with activity. In the Bible God says to us, "Be still, and know that I am God" (Ps. 46:11). More than physical stillness, it is mental and emotional stillness. It is walking away from the business that may not be completed by sundown on Friday. It is taking those deadlines that are pressing in on us and shelving them for twenty-five hours. It is saying NO to the push and YES to the peace. YES to the *shalom*.

TRUE REST REFLECTS TRUST

I'm sure you have heard the expression "taking a sabbatical." A sabbatical is usually an indefinite leave or departure from something (e.g., job, school). Notice how closely related the word *sabbatical* is to *Sabbath*. Its Greek and Latin origins mean "of the Sabbath."

The idea of the *Shabbat* is also connected to the sabbatical year, the *shmitta* year. This connection to *shmitta* is the most countercultural aspect of *Shabbat*. God says not only take one day off a week but to take *one year off* from farming the ground **every seven years.**

> For six years you may sow your field and for six years you may prune your vineyard and gather in its fruits. But in the seventh year there is to be a *Shabbat* [Sabbath] rest for the land—a *Shabbat* to ADONAI. (Lev. 25:3–4)

Even the land must rest. Now, think about it—no work for an entire year. No work usually translates into no income. How do you *rest* and not wrestle with that instruction? It's called Trust with a capital *T*.

We can go a step further and realize that every fifty years is the Year of Jubilee. During this unique year there is not only rest from farming the land, but debts are completely forgiven (given a permanent rest). In biblical times, slaves were able to return to the area from which they came and to their families.

The Bible tells us that you can't please God without faith. Well, you can't please Him without trust either. Trust requires that we know and understand His heart and nature. When we don't trust Him, we are not believing Him when He calls

Himself by His many names: *Adonai-Tzva'ot* (our Protector), *Adonai-Rapha* (our Healer), *Adonai-Yireh* (our Provider). In the book of Jeremiah, Israel goes into exile because the people fail to keep the sabbatical year and the Year of Jubilee. Why? They did not rest and trust the Provider to provide. We can enter His rest when we trust God.

THE JEWISH SECRET TO SUCCESS

Rabbi Yitzchok Adlerstein likens the Sabbath to "a week in Hawaii without ever leaving home."[1] The *Shabbat* is a precious time and a treasure from God.

A well-known Jewish philosopher by the name of Ehad Ha-am said, "It is not so much that the Jews have kept the *Shabbat*, but the *Shabbat* has kept the Jews." This statement is the absolute truth (*emes* in Hebrew). *Shabbat* is one of the secrets as to why the Jewish people have not only survived even in the great times of peril and persecution but have thrived collectively against all the odds.

> Keep the *Shabbat*, because it is holy for you. . . . Work is to be done for six days, but on the seventh day is a *Shabbat* of complete rest, holy to ADONAI. . . . So *Bnei-Yisrael* is to keep the *Shabbat*, to observe the *Shabbat* throughout their generations as a perpetual covenant. It is a sign between Me and *Bnei-Yisrael* forever, for in six days ADONAI made heaven and earth, and on

---

1 Yitzchok, Alderstein, "A Weekly Trip to Hawaii," *Jewish Action*, Spring 2012, https://jewishaction.com/religion/shabbat-holidays/a-weekly-trip-to-hawaii/.

the seventh day He ceased from work and rested. (Ex. 31:14–17)

Shabbat is an oasis in the midst of the desert of time that refreshes and rejuvenates our body and soul. God Himself rested on the *Shabbat*, not because He was tired but because He wanted to model for us its great importance. Concerning this the Bible says, "On the seventh day He [God] ceased from work and rested," or more literally in Hebrew "resouled" (Ex. 31:17). After a long week, we are like our favorite pair of shoes whose heels get run down from all the wear and tear of life's busyness. But taking a *Shabbat* resouls us like putting new soles on our favorite pair of shoes!

You might ask how *Shabbat* has preserved the Jewish people. When you look at the ritual of *Shabbat*, it will make more sense to you. I will summarize some of the elements here and then outline step-by-step the ritual at the end of this chapter.

As you now know, we first stop all the work connected with the world. We focus spiritually, emotionally, and relationally. *Shabbat* brings *shalom* into our homes and our lives and also brings a *b'rachot*, a blessing. Another name by which God refers to Himself? *Adonai-Shalom*, our perfect peace.

We begin the traditional *Shabbat* dinner by singing the *Shalom Alecheim*, asking God to send His angels to bring us the blessing of peace. We then **speak** blessings over each other. This is significant. Proverbs 18:21 tells us that "death and life are in the **control of the tongue**." We lay hands on our children as Jacob laid his hands on the sons of Joseph to impart to the next generation. We speak a blessing over them, telling them how much we love and appreciate them.

There is no greater joy in my home than after we light the *Shabbat* candles and we sing *Shabbat Shalom*. My family cozily gathers, and dance erupts throughout our whole home. When my sons were young we played a game called *Shabbat* tag; we would hold one of our sons, and we would run after each other as we sang *Shabbat* songs. This fun reminds us God created us for play. Remember that "He who sits in heaven laughs!" (Ps. 2:4).

The joy of the Lord truly is our strength when we can enter into rest by enjoying the playfulness programmed into our DNA by our heavenly Father.

We also make sure to honor our wives and mothers by reading Proverbs 31. Then we speak a personal blessing over them because, in Jewish thought, women are the reason blessing comes to a home. First Peter 3:7 admonishes, "If we fight with our wives and do not honor them, it hinders our prayers in heaven" (my paraphrase). During *Shabbat* dinner in my home, the wives read Psalm 112 and offer a personal blessing to their husbands to honor them and create an atmosphere of *shalom* in the home. It is also our tradition for the children to bless their parents and grandparents. The Proverbs verse above about the power of the spoken word ("death and life are in the control of the tongue") ends with "those who indulge in it will eat its fruit." The survival of the Jews amid extreme adversity throughout the ages IS the fruit of these spoken *Shabbat* blessings.

The Promise of Remembrance . . . START HERE

WHY A GARDEN?

How many of us get stressed in a garden? I don't imagine seeing many hands raised. Why was Eden a garden? The garden is a symbol of rest. God placed us in a garden where it was a seven-days-a-week *Shabbat*, not just *Shabbat* on the seventh day. It was a place of *shalom* and delight. God designed us for delight—us in Him and Him in us. The purpose of creation is for us to encounter God—Creator with the created, the Lover with the beloved, the Source of joy to be enjoyed, served, and worshiped by us, the beneficiaries. In John 17:3, Jesus tells us, "This is eternal life, that they may know You, the only true God." In Jewish thought, God didn't need to create anything. But He is Love, and Love needs to be expressed in relationship with something *to* love. Therefore, He created man and woman, the crown of His creation.

Shabbat returns us to Eden. It allows us to remember where we came from and where we are returning to. It reminds us of our true identity. We are spiritual beings having a physical experience and not the other way around.

*Un*rest entered after the Fall. After the transgression of Adam and Eve, man had to toil to eat. The six days of the week in which we work by the sweat of our brow belong to the secular. The seventh day, the *Shabbat*, belongs to the spiritual. It brings us back to the garden, to delight in the Designer and each other, to experience Eden-like peace and *shalom*. Even during exile, slavery, persecution, the *Shabbat* reminded us that we were not slaves of Pharaoh but were children of the King. God told Moses to command Pharaoh: "Let My people go, so they may serve Me" (Ex. 9). We are not called to be slaves or servants, but we are called to be sons and daughters. Observing *Shabbat* through the ages has freed us from the ordinary and the suffering. When we don't observe *Shabbat*, when we are too busy to rest and remember, it is like returning to Egypt, in bondage to the pharaohs of schedules, money, career, materialism.

We become human *doings* instead of human beings. We gain our value from what we do rather than who we are. Think of how Jesus addressed the situation with Martha and Mary. Martha was busy *doing* her duties as a hostess. However, Mary chose to be at the feet of Jesus, to spend time with Him. Jesus responded by saying, "Martha, Martha, you are anxious and bothered about many things; **but only one thing is necessary. For Miriam [Mary] has chosen the good part,** which will not be taken away from her" (Luke 10:41–42). In other words, honoring the *Shabbat* stills us to be with the Lord and each other. It helps us remember our humanity and the relational intimacy for which we were created.

SET APART

Do you remember a time when stores were closed on Sundays? It was a day set apart for *solemn assembly*[2] and family and friends. Our culture used to honor the Sabbath. I'm reminded of *Chariots of Fire* when Eric Liddell sees the children playing soccer on the Sabbath. He says, "Not on the Lord's day."

2 Leviticus 23:36.

Sadly, the Lord's day has become like any other day. Candidly, it is our loss when everything feels the same. There's a sense of excitement and anticipation when something is set apart as unique. That is why we frequently save our best clothes for the *Shabbat*. We keep our best food for the *Shabbat* dinner because we want to treat it as unique, as the gift that God gave to us.

In addition to taking the necessary time, we honor *Shabbat* by speaking the blessings over each other as well as make *kiddush* over the wine or grape juice. *Kiddush* means to sanctify. Making *kiddush* over the wine or juice sanctifies the *Shabbat*. We fill the cup to the brim because we remember that God is a God of abundance. We bless Him who brings forth fruit from the earth. We speak this blessing as a remembrance of the work of creation and how God has chosen to redeem us from our modern-day Egypts as He did the Israelites from ancient Egypt.

THE FEAST OF FEASTS

Let us be glad and rejoice, and let us give honor to Him.
For the time has come for the wedding feast of the Lamb,
and His bride has prepared herself.
Revelation 19:7 NLT

We know that one of the focuses of *Shabbat* is to remember. But the *Shabbat* dinner also causes us to anticipate, to look forward—*Shabbat* is a foretaste of the wedding banquet we will eat with the Messiah in a time to come. The Jewish people feast on *Shabbat* as we sit down around the communal table to celebrate. The feast is like the rehearsal dinner before the wedding. It reminds us of our Bridegroom King. It also shows that God likes to party, and joy is a fruit of the Spirit. Delighting in God and each other is a form of worship. It is what we were designed to do, as in the garden.

This God party also feeds the soul and spirit as well as the body. By overlooking *Shabbat*, we cheat ourselves of spiritual nourishment. We also deny our children our parental blessing as well as allowing them to come to know God as joyous and childlike.

OUR SPIRITUAL ID

Yet for a little while you made them only
a little lower than the angels
and crowned them with glory and honor.
You gave them authority over all things.
Hebrews 2:7–8 NLT

Our great worth in God is a crucial focus of remembrance during *Shabbat*. We remember the work of creation over five days in which God created the world. Man and woman were His final act of creation on the sixth day. Humanity is the crown, the pinnacle of God's creation. Individual interpretations of Hebrews 2, which references Psalm 8, pronounce man as a little lower than God. Part of Satan's rebellion, which targets man, is because of this spiritual hierarchy.

He calls us to Himself during the divine, weekly date to remind us that we are created in His image and crowned with glory and honor. This calling from God gives us inherent worth and value. His calling is our spiritual ID and is unshakable. The only way not to waver from our true identity is to spend the time resting and remembering.

By creating us in His image, we were designed to co-partner with God in creation. Just as God sculpted us out of dirt and clay, God wants us to take the raw goods of creation and to build something incredible. We are to bring forth children, to cultivate the land—we were created to create. The Lord calls us to partner with Him and includes us in His plan for developing, transforming, and redeeming the world.

Prosper! Reproduce! Fill Earth! Take **charge**!
Be responsible for fish in the sea and birds in the air, for every living thing that moves on the face of Earth. (Gen. 1:26, my paraphrase)

Another aspect to co-partnering in creation is being good stewards of God's goods. God gives man, the crown of creation, the authority to be fruitful, multiply, and have dominion over creation. We often mistake this dominion as domination. However, the authority given us means good stewardship and not reckless disregard. We are to treat this honor that God has bestowed upon us with reciprocal respect, which will benefit all life around us.

The Promise of Restoration . . .

RELATIONAL INTIMACY

The Bible exhorts us in the book of Ephesians to "make the most of [our] time because the days are evil" (5:16). We know how the demands of each day can consume our time and our energy. Without boundaries, we are swallowed whole. *Shabbat* is about corralling the runaway stallion of time for the *restoration* of relationship with God and others. All that matters this side of eternity is relationships—first with God and then with our fellow man. Relational intimacy is everything.

What eulogy has talked about how much someone has in their 401(k), or their IRA or bank account? When recalling a lost loved one, people talk about how they felt about the person, memories of times together—relationship.

God intends for *Shabbat* to also remind us of His redeeming work. Redemption or restoration, in a sense, is tied to the work of creation—a new creation. Redemption is the restoration of something that was lost and is now regained or restored. The blessings of peace, *shalom*, delight, and relational intimacy with God that were lost in the Fall are restored through the work of redemption. We are returned to the garden.

THE PART SANCTIFIES THE WHOLE

Imagine the seven days of the week are like the seven branches of the *menorah*. *Shabbat* is the middle branch, with three branches on each side. It radiates life, blessing, and holiness both backward and forward. The center sanctifies that on either side of it, or the part sanctifies the whole. Observing *Shabbat* on the seventh day of the week sanctifies the other six days of the week in Jewish thought.

As the center is often the focal point, *Shabbat* focuses our thoughts on the messianic age to come—*Yom Shekulo Shabbat*—in which *Shabbat* is seven days a week and not just the seventh day. Again, it restores us to the garden. *Shabbat* is a taste of the messianic age, which will be one long Sabbath!

YESHUA AND *SHABBAT*
What Did Jesus Do?

Yeshua celebrated the *Shabbat*. In Matthew and Luke, He goes into the temple and reads from the *Torah* scrolls. In fact, in Matthew 12, Yeshua calls Himself the Lord of the *Shabbat*:

> But I tell you that something greater than the Temple is here. . . . For the Son of Man is Lord of the *Shabbat*. (Matt. 12:6, 8)

So, when we honor *Shabbat*, we are honoring Yeshua. The disciples also continued to honor the *Shabbat* after Yeshua ascended.

TORAH MIND TWISTER

We know that *Shabbat* points to creation and redemption, ultimately pointing to the work of Yeshua. If you're game for a mini Hebrew lesson, I think you will find the information

I'm about to share with you very interesting, further illuminating Yeshua in *Shabbat*.

Aleph is the first letter of the Hebrew alphabet and mainly begins the many names of God—*Adonai, El Shaddai, Elohim, El Roi*. These are some of the divine names that all start with an *Aleph*. However, the **first** letter of the **first** word in the **first** chapter of the *Torah* (Gen. 1) is the **second** letter of the Hebrew alphabet. It is the letter *Bet*. As every letter in the Hebrew alphabet also represents a number, the letter *Bet* also stands for the number *two*. Sages ask the question: Why does the second letter begin the *Torah*?

The first two words beginning the *Torah* in Genesis 1, starting with the letter *Bet*, are *Beresheit bara*. *Beresheit* can mean God created the world "through His firstborn." Traditional rabbis believe the *firstborn* can mean the *Torah* or the Messiah yet to come. The spiritual significance of the *Torah* beginning with *Bet* for us as followers of the Messiah is that it also opens the word *Ben*, or "son," who is *firstborn* of the Father and is the Second Person (number two) of the Godhead. We, as believers in Yeshua, believe what is supported by Hebrews 1 and John 1. We believe original creation comes **through** the Son and new creation comes **through** the Son, the Messiah, who has already come and will come again.

Beresheit can also mean the world was created "on account of the firstborn." This interpretation of the word points to the redemption aspect of *Shabbat*—God as Redeemer. Before God created the world, He knew of the Fall. The Messiah was willing to suffer to undo the effects of the Fall before the world existed. Father and Son made a divine deal. This divine deal is the reason Revelation 13:8 calls Jesus "the **Lamb slain** from the foundation of the world" (NKJV).

In other words, God made sure the antidote preceded the sickness. God created the world *through* the Messiah, *on account* of the Messiah, and the Messiah would save His creation.

Shabbat finds its ultimate fulfillment of creation and redemption in Messiah Yeshua. God is the same yesterday, today, and forever (Heb. 13:8). By celebrating *Shabbat*, we are remembering not only what God did in the past but what He is still doing in the present through His *Ben*, His Son, the Architect of Creation and the Author of redemption.

HOW TO CELEBRATE
Shabbat

1. **Preparing for *Shabbat*:**

Gather your *Shabbat* supplies as early on Friday (or even Thursday) as you can. After sundown on Friday, you do no work. You will need at least two candlestick holders and at least two candles that are unscented and may or may not be colored. Also, purchase two loaves of *challah* bread, a Jewish egg bread that is soft and slightly sweet. You will  also need a Kosher bottle of wine or grape juice and glasses for everyone who is celebrating.

Prepare the *Shabbat* table. On your main dining room table, place the two candles in their candlestick holders. Put the two loaves of *challah* on a plate and cover them with a cloth if you don't have a *challah* cover. Open the wine and have the glasses ready. Do all of this before sundown.

2. ***Hadlakat Nerot* (Candle Lighting)**

Light the candles. Just before sundown, ideally eighteen minutes before sunset, have the woman of the house light the candles in silence. Candle lighting is a time for reflection. After a moment or two of thought, the lighter of the candles recites the prayer over the candles: *Baruch Atah Adonai Eloheinu Melech ha'olam asher kidshanu bemitzvotav vetzivanu lehadlik ner shel Shabbat*. This prayer is thanking God, Creator of the universe, for the blessing of the light from the candles.

3. Sing *Shalom Aleikhem*

The purpose of *Shabbat* is to create *shalom* in the home. We do this by asking God to send His angels of peace by singing this song.

4. *Birkhot Ha-Mishpachah* (Blessing the Family)

If you have children, bless the children first. If they are male, you say: *Yesimcha Elohim ke-Efrayim vechi-Menasheh*. This blessing means "May you be like Ephraim and Manasseh, two hon-

orable patriarchs from the *Torah*." If they are female, you say: "*Yesimech Elohim ke-Sarah Rivkah Rachel ve-Leah*." This blessing means "May you be like Sarah, Rebekah, Rachel, and Leah, four honorable matriarchs from the *Torah*." Then bless all the children with the Aaronic benediction found in Numbers 6:24–26. Following this, the husband blesses his wife and the other women at the table by reading Proverbs 31:10–31, known in Hebrew as *Eishet Chayil*. The wife then blesses the husband and the other men at the table by reading Psalm 112, known in Hebrew as *Ashrei Ish*, "Blessed is the man."

5. *Kiddush* (Sanctification of the Day)

By reciting the *Kiddush*, we declare the holiness of the *Shabbat* day and remember God as the Creator and Redeemer of all, by blessing the cup of grape juice or wine. Pour the wine or grape juice into the cups. Raise your cup and recite Genesis 1:31—2:3. Then you recite the following blessing: *Baruch Atah Adonai Eloheinu Melech ha'olam borei peri hagafen.* This prayer gives thanks to God, the Creator of the universe, for the fruit of the vine. There is a third blessing found in all traditional prayer books known as *Mekadesh ha-Shabbat*:

Blessed are You, Lord, our God, King of the universe, who sanctifies us with His commandments, and has been pleased with us. You have lovingly and willingly given us Your holy Shabbat as an inheritance, in memory of cre-ation. The Shabbat is the first among our holy days and a remembrance of our exodus from Egypt. Indeed, You have chosen us and made us holy among all peoples and have willingly and lovingly given us Your holy Shabbat for an inheritance. Blessed are You, who sanctifies the Shabbat. Amen.

After the blessing, everyone is to take a sip of the wine.

6. *Netilat Yadayin* (Washing of the Hands)

In the days of the temple, the priests and rabbis would ritually cleanse their hands to signify the fact that they were partaking of a holy meal. We pour water three times over each hand and recite the following blessing: *Barukh atah Adonai, Elohaynu, melekh ha-olam, asher kid'shanu b'mitzvotav, v'tzivanu al n'tilat yadayim.* "Blessed are You, Lord, our God, King of the universe, who sanctifies us with His commandments, and commands us concerning washing of hands."

7. *HaMotzi* (Blessing over the Bread)

The blessing over the two loaves of *challah* reminds us of the double portion of *manna* that God gave us in the wilderness. It also reminds us of the two tablets of the Ten Commandments. And, for us as followers of the Messiah, it reminds us that He is the Bread of Life who came once and

who will return again. Bless the bread. Take the cover off the *challah* and raise the two loaves of bread in your hands and recite the following blessing: *Baruch Atah Adonai Eloheinu Melech ha'olam hamotzi lechem min ha'aretz.* This is a prayer  thanking God, Creator of the universe, for bringing forth bread from the earth. Tear a small piece of bread from the loaf, dip it in salt, and give a small piece to everyone to eat.

8. *Seudat Shabbat* (The *Shabbat* Meal)

On *Shabbat*, we feast together as a family to remind us of three things:

- The goodness of God and the blessing of Creation
- That we are no longer slaves in Egypt but free men and women
- A foretaste of the coming messianic banquet

At this point, the pre-meal blessings have been said and you are now instructed to eat your *Shabbat* evening meal. After the meal, a member of the party may want to recite the *Birkat Hamazon* prayer. It can be found in any Jewish prayer book and joining in is encouraged.

9. *Z'mirot* (*Shabbat* Songs)

During the *Shabbat* meal, it is customary to sing songs of thanks and praise unto the Lord. (You can refer to our *Shabbat Table Guide* for songs and other information about celebrating *Shabbat*. Visit fusionglobal.org for your copy.)

10. *Birkat Ha-Mazon* (Blessing after the Meal)

To complete our *Shabbat* dinner, we thank God for providing us with the delicious food, family, and friends as well as the gift of *Shabbat* itself. The blessing after the meal is inspired from Deuteronomy 8:10 as God commands, "So you will eat and be full, and you will bless ADONAI your God." The grace after the meals begins by reciting Psalm 126, followed by a fourfold blessing, which can be found in most prayer books or searching on the internet for *Birkat Ha-Mazon*.

A FEW CLOSING THOUGHTS

To be clear, do not feel pressure to say all the traditional Sabbath blessings in Hebrew or even English, but rather take the time to bless and be blessed. Don't confuse form with function. Be creative and use the order of the traditional *Shabbat* as a guide. Make your own family traditions, and please add or even substitute your own personal blessings or Scripture verses. Celebrating *Shabbat* is not an all-or-nothing thing, especially for followers of the Messiah who are new to it.

Remember, *Shabbat* is meant to be not a burden but a blessing! So have fun, be creative, and don't put pressure on yourself or others to do it the perfect and correct way. And although *Shabbat* is traditionally done on Friday night, you can incorporate these principles into any meal. For my Gentile Christian friends, that might mean a Sunday supper. Look at *Shabbat* not as obligation but as an invitation to go deeper spiritually and relationally. *Shabbat* will be a new journey for many of you, so take it slow and easy, and enjoy each small step you take along the way. And what is true of *Shabbat* is true of all the biblical holidays.

My hope and prayer for you is that you grow to love the Sabbath and all the holidays as much as my family and I do, make it a regular part of your life, and share its joy and blessing with others.

You can find the full service with the blessings in a resource I put together called *Created for Connection: A Sabbath Supper Club Guide*. It's a practical guide that walks you through a *Shabbat* dinner. It includes all the blessings and will equip you and your family to experience the blessing of the Sabbath. You can find yours at our website: https://www.fusionglobal.org/shop/sabbath-supper-club-guide/.

Passover is foundational to every part of Jewish life. The remembrance of the exodus out of Egypt is the foundation of the Jewish holidays. In many ways, it is also foundational to all of Jewish spirituality and much of Jewish practice.

CHAPTER TWO

PASSOVER

*"It is the **Passover** sacrifice to the* LORD,

for he passed over the houses of the Israelites in Egypt.

And though he struck the Egyptians,

he spared our families." When Moses had finished speaking,

all the people bowed down to the ground and worshiped.

Exodus 12:27 NLT

THE LAST *SEDER,* NOT THE LAST SUPPER

I wrote in the Preface that every milestone in Jesus' life occurred on a *chag,* a Jewish holiday. His death was no exception. Yeshua-Jesus died during Passover. He is called the Passover Lamb. Before His death, He dined with His disciples in what is known as the Last Supper. This was a Last *Seder.* He was observing Passover by having a traditional dinner called a *seder* with His closest friends.

The most famous icon of the Last Supper is the painting by Leonardo da Vinci. Jesus and His very Western European–looking disciples are gathering around a rectangular table with glasses of wine and loaves of fluffy white bread. There is NO WAY such a thing as these leavened loaves sat on Jesus' *seder* table. Passover is also known as the Feast of *Unleavened* Bread. The large, flat cracker called *matzah* is the only type of bread eaten during this holiday. Why? The answer is in the backstory of Passover.

The Promise of Redemption . . .

PASSED OVER

Passover is foundational to every part of Jewish life. The remembrance of the exodus out of Egypt is the foundation of the Jewish holidays. In many ways, it is also foundational to all of Jewish spirituality and much of Jewish practice.

Passover always begins with the *maggid,* the telling of the story. When the story is spoken, it is told in the present tense and as if it happened to us, not our ancestors. The *seder* is intended to do the following:

- Raise questions and make the night different and stand out from any other celebration or event
- Engage us, our children, and our senses so that we can actively pass the knowledge of God from generation to generation.

One of the main purposes of Passover is to make disciples.

The year is 1446 BC, and the Hebrew people have been plagued by the Egyptians and trapped in slavery for several generations. God has heard the cries of their hearts, and Moses is His man to set them free. Pharaoh proves unwilling to let his slaves go and cause an economic downturn for his country. In reaction to Pharaoh's decision, God plagues the Egyptians in ten different ways, the tenth plague being the death of the first-born son in all the Egyptians households.

Passover, or *Pesach* in Hebrew, literally means to "skip over," referring to the angel of death who skipped or *passed over* the Hebrew households marked by the lambs' blood on their door-ways. Finally, Pharaoh cries "uncle," and the people of Israel are free to go. God instructs them to hit the road in haste. So, they bake their bread quickly, not allowing it to rise, which is why unleavened bread, *matzah,* is eaten throughout this holiday. Do you see why dinner rolls on da Vinci's table don't accurately portray the Last Supper/*seder* of our Lord?

But, there is another reason why we do not eat leaven at the Passover. Jewish sages teach that leaven, *chametz,* symbolizes sin and the evil inclination. This symbolism and reference to sin is what Paul is referring to in 1 Corinthians 5:8: "Therefore let us keep the Festival, not with the old bread **leavened** with malice and wickedness, but with the unleavened bread of sincerity and truth" (NIV).

SPRING CLEANING, JEWISH STYLE

Several days before the Passover, there is an elaborate preparation of cleaning the house from top to bottom, removing all leaven. In my home, we still prepare for the Passover in this way. My sons, Avi and Judah, join in because the children have a responsibility to help their parents cleanse the house of leaven to purify it in preparation for the Passover. Many wives love this time of year because it is the only time the entire family joins in for the deep cleaning required. It is customary to vacuum every corner of the house and scrub every cabinet. It is traditional even to have special Passover dishes that do not come into contact with leaven. If I use the same metal utensils, for example, I boil them in water to *kasher* them before the start of Passover. I put hot water over our counters to purify them. If not, it's traditional to put aluminum foil, plastic, or something over them. There can be no crumbs in the corners of the pockets of clothing. I also go through my car to make sure that there is not even a little bit of leaven left.

Yeshua-Jesus entered the temple to expose the leaven—the impurities and the injustices happening within its walls. Instead of vacuuming, He overturned the tables of the moneychangers in the court of the Gentiles. The Jerusalem temple was His Father's house. He was a good Son, cleaning out His Father's house.

If you are presenting your offering upon the altar, and there remember that your brother has something against you, leave your offering there before the altar and go. First be reconciled to your brother, and then come and present your offering. (Matt. 5:23–24)

Matthew is quoting Yeshua-Jesus as He talked about leaven within our spiritual temple. When we have grudges, unforgiveness, bitterness, disputes with others, all of that is the leaven that can grow into sin. Jesus is telling us to get rid of it, clean it out, and come to the altar with unleavened hearts, if you will, to offer our gifts. When we partake of the Passover meal as well as communion, we need our inner dwelling place purified as much as we have purified our homes.

THE MEANING OF THE *MATZAH*

You shall eat no leavened bread with it; seven days you
shall eat unleavened bread with it, that is, the bread
of affliction (for you came out of the land of Egypt in
haste), that you may remember the day in which you
came out of the land of Egypt all the days of your life.
Deuteronomy 16:3 NKJV

Matzah bread has almost a corrugated look, with holes like dotted lines running vertically alongside rows of browned pockets of dough that form peaks and valleys. The affliction that the bread represents is the centuries of slavery in Egypt endured by the Hebrews. The brown stripes running the length of the bread recall the lashings of the slave drivers upon our enslaved ancestors. It is also known as the bread of "freedom and healing," when God redeemed them from Egypt with an "outstretched arm" (Ex. 6:6). We can also see Yeshua represented in the *matzah*. Isaiah 53 tells us:

> Surely he took up our pain and bore our suffering, yet we considered him punished by God, stricken by him, and afflicted. But he was pierced for our transgressions . . . the punishment that brought us peace was on him, and by his wounds we are healed. (vv. 4–5 NIV)

Yeshua's bread of affliction was the weight of our sins. The *matzah*'s holes stand for His piercings, and the brown stripes represent His stripes by which we are healed and set free from bondage to sin and our own Egypts. These are personal prisons that confine and limit us from being who God wants us to be and doing what He has destined for us.

The fourth step in the *seder* is called *yachatz*, which means "to break." At this point in the meal, the *matzah* is broken. During the Last *Seder*, *matzah* was the bread Jesus lifted, broke, and "gave . . . to his disciples, saying, 'Take and eat; this is my body'" (Matt. 26:26 NIV). In fact, communion is looked upon as a mini-Passover each time we partake.

Did you ever think there was such deep meaning in so thin a cracker?

FOUR CUPS

There were four decrees that Pharaoh made against the Hebrew people: (1) They "made their lives bitter with hard labor" (Ex. 4:14). (2) "If it's a son, then kill him" (Ex. 4:16). (3) "Cast every son that is born into the river" (Ex. 4:22). (4) "You are not to give the people any more straw to make bricks" (Ex. 5:7).

The four cups of the *seder* meal symbolize the four distinct promises God made to the people of Israel in Exodus 6:6–7 that **counteract** Pharaoh's four decrees.

> Therefore, say to the Israelites: "I am the LORD, and I will bring you out from under the yoke of the Egyptians. I will free you from being slaves to them, and I will redeem you with an outstretched arm and with mighty acts of judgment. I will take you as my own people, and I will be your God. Then you will know that I am the LORD your God, who brought you out from under the yoke of the Egyptians." (NIV)

These promises represent the four stages of redemption. The first cup, known as the cup of sanctification, corresponds to "I will bring you out." We respond, "God, make us holy. . . . Set us apart for Your plans and holy purposes for our lives."

The second cup is the cup of deliverance: "I will free you." This second cup is also known as the cup of plagues—we remember that God did not just redeem, but He redeemed us with great signs and great wonders. We remember that God, through Moses, turned water into blood and that the Messiah's first miracle turned water into wine.

The third cup is the cup of redemption: "I will redeem you." It reminds us of the blood of the Passover lamb that the Israelites put upon the doorposts of their houses. This cup is also known as the cup of the Messiah, and we remember Yeshua is the ultimate Passover Lamb.

The fourth cup is the cup of acceptance or thanksgiving: "I will take you as my own people" because we say it over the psalms of praise known as *Hallel*. It looks to the future, to the coming of the Kingdom. It was over the fourth cup that Yeshua said, "I will never drink of this fruit of the vine from now on, until that day when I drink it anew with you in My Father's kingdom" (Matt. 26:29). We acknowledge and give thanks for our acceptance as children of the King, knowing our position, power, and authority in the Messiah.

THE NUMBER FOUR

I've come to realize that God loves numbers. Nothing is random in the Bible, not even the numbers. The number *seven* stands for perfection and completion—seven days in which God created the earth. The number *three* stands for the Godhead—three in one. Yeshua-Jesus' ministry lasted on earth three and a half years, and His time in the tomb was three days. His lifetime was a multiple of three: He was thirty-three years old at the time of His death.

Biblically, the number four epitomizes exile and redemption. We've seen above how four connects to redemption. The four cups also point to the reality that Israel was going to experience four exiles: Babylonian, Persian, Greek, and Roman. These were not only physical exiles but also emotional and spiritual ones caused by physical exiles, as you will see in an upcoming chapter.

Yeshua, as the Passover Lamb, came to undo these four aspects of exile. The first aspect he came to deal with is spiritual exile. We were spiritually exiled from God when we sinned in the garden. Yeshua took this separation onto Himself on the cross, saying, "My God, my God, why have you forsaken me?" (Matt. 27:46 NIV). We are exiled from one another. On the cross, He delivered us from this interpersonal exile when He said, "Forgive them, for they do not know what they are doing. . . . Today you shall be with Me in Paradise" (Luke 23:34, 43). We are interpersonally exiled, emotionally and psychologically, from our true selves and our destinies as sons and daughters of God. Yeshua reversed this exile as the apostle John reflected in his Gospel, "But whoever did receive Him, those trusting in His name, to these He gave the right to become children of God" (John 1:12). The fourth exile is the physical exile, as the ground and all creation was cursed because of the Fall. The thorns piercing His head represent His taking this physical curse upon Himself on the cross to undo the deed of Adam and Eve.

From the four corners of the earth, from every direction, God is going to redeem His people. There are four cups of catastrophe that the nations will have to drink and four cups of consolation that will be given to Israel at the great redemption, the final redemption (Isa. 11:12).

Four Hebrew letters form the name of God—*Yud, Hey, Vav, Hey*—which we pronounce as *Adonai*. There are ONLY four letters in God's name to signify that ALL of God was involved in the process of redemption. God did not send an intermediary; God Himself came and redeemed us from *four* hundred years of enslavement. God and no other parted the sea and led us across onto dry land.

BITTER AND SWEET

The bitter herbs that are part of the *seder* meal represent the bitterness of slavery. There is *maror, charoset,* and *karpas.* The *maror* is usually raw horseradish that stands for the harshness of the Egyptian oppression of the Hebrews. The *maror* is dipped in *charoset,* a sweet-tasting mixture of apples, nuts, cinnamon, and wine, which symbolizes the mortar used by the people of Israel for building during their slavery. The *charoset* exemplifies how God can turn what is bitter into something sweet as Romans 8:28 reminds us: "God causes everything to work together for the good of those who love God and are called according to his purpose for them" (NLT). The *karpas* is parsley, meant to recall the hyssop that was used to apply the blood to the doorposts of the house. We dip it in saltwater to remember the tears of our ancestors and the sweat of our brow in Egypt. Some say the salty water represents the Red Sea, which God parted for us through the staff of Moses.

However, there is another aspect to this herb. Royalty used parsley in the multi-course banquet meals. It cleansed the palette between the servings of the different dishes. The parsley serves to remind us of our royalty. We are children of the King. A man once came to a rabbi and asked, "What is the worst sin in the world?" The rabbi said, "If you forget you are a child of the King." The man then asked, "What is the second worst sin?" The rabbi said, "To know that you are a child of the King and not live like one."

God, the King of the universe, created us in His image. Jesus, the King of kings, regained our royal inheritance for us that was lost in the Fall.

"And He raised us up with Him and **seated** us with Him in the heavenly places in Messiah *Yeshua*" (Eph. 2:6).

YESHUA AS THE GREATER MOSES

There has never been another prophet in Israel like Moses, whom the LORD knew face to face. The LORD sent him to perform all the miraculous signs and wonders in the land of Egypt against Pharaoh."
Deuteronomy 34:10–11 NLT

Yeshua as the greater Moses might be a new concept to you, but it is biblically sound, and I'd like to explore this idea. Deuteronomy 34 says two things that made Moses unique: God spoke to him face-to-face, and he performed matchless signs and wonders when he delivered Israel out of Egypt. One of the ways that God spoke to Moses was through the burning bush. The book of Hebrews tells us it was not an ordinary bush. It was a very particular type of bush God revealed Himself in—a thorn bush. Why did God reveal Himself to Moses in a thorn bush? Thorns represent affliction, suffering, and pain.

God is saying to Moses, "I have seen your pain. I have seen your suffering. I have seen what has been happening to you for these hundreds of years, and I identify with you. I understand what you have been through, and it breaks My heart." It was compassion that moved Him to redeem His people, causing Moses to tell Israel that God had remembered their prayers and He cared for them.

What encircled the head of the King of kings when He hung on the cross? An intertwining of thorns served as His crown, which also signifies the Fall in Genesis 3:18, where "**thorns** and thistles will sprout for you." He took the affliction of the sin of the man; He absorbed all the pain and suffering meant for us and came to undo the curse of creation. He took the fall for the Fall. He allowed Himself to be put upon a tree (cross) to restore what had been taken from the tree.

Moses' unique relationship with God is also demonstrated by the fact that he could regularly enter into the Holy of Holies. Only a high priest could enter and only once a year on *Yom Kippur*. When Yeshua, the unique Son of God, died upon the cross, the curtain separating the Holy of Holies was torn in two, allowing all to enter and ending the separation between God and man.

Another correlation between Moses and Jesus is the ninth plague. There were three days of darkness over Egypt. When Jesus hung on the cross, there were three hours of darkness between the sixth and ninth hour. The tenth plague was the death of the firstborn son in all the Egyptian households. The angel passed over the houses of the Israelites, which were marked by the lambs' blood. Yeshua-Jesus is God's firstborn Son, and His blood, the blood of the Lamb, allows us to pass over from death to eternal life.

Moses' first miracle when he was delivering Israel from Egypt was to turn the water into blood. Yeshua-Jesus' first public miracle at the start of His ministry of redemption was to turn the water into wine. The result was a wine so fine that the wedding guests commented that the best was saved usually for drinking last. Jesus, as the greater Moses, did not come to bring death; rather, He came "that they might have life, and have it abundantly!" (John 10:10).

Jesus, the greater Moses, the Passover Lamb, delivers us into the Promised Land.

THE *HAGGADAH* AND THE STEPS OF THE *Seder*

The Passover *seder* (a Jewish ritual dinner) is based on the *haggadah*, a book of instructions, prayers, blessings, and stories that lays out the proper order for the ritual. *Haggadah* means "the telling," referring to the recitation of the Exodus story, one of the essential aspects of the *seder*. We read in the *Pesach Haggadah*, "In each and every generation, a person is obligated to see himself as if he left Egypt."[1]

The basic text of the traditional *haggadah* is almost identical to that used in the eleventh century. However, in the 1960s and 1970s, many different versions began to appear. Today there are hundreds of *haggadot* (the plural of *haggadah*) available, each revealing the same basic ritual but with a different spin.

Each *seder* needs a leader, someone who will conduct the proceedings and read key parts of the *haggadah*. In traditional homes, the leader may wear a white *kittel*. This unique robe is worn only during certain rituals to create the awareness that this is a sacred time: the *seder*, *Yom Kippur*, one's wedding, and

---

1 Pesach Haggadah (Magid: Rabban Gamliel's Three Things). For full text see https://www.sefaria.org/Pesach_Haggadah%2C_Rabban_Gamliel's_Three_Things?lang=bi.

one's burial. The *seder* then proceeds through its fifteen steps done in the following order:

1. *Kadesh*: Recite *Kiddush*, first cup of wine
2. *U'rchatz*: Washing of your hands without a blessing
3. *Karpas*: The appetizer—dip green herbs into salt water, eat
4. *Yachatz*: Breaking of the middle *matzah*
5. *Maggid*: Tell the story of the Exodus, second cup of wine
6. *Rachtzah*: Wash your hands, with blessing
7. *Motzi*: Blessing of the unleavened bread
8. *Matzah*: *Matzah* is eaten
9. *Maror*: Bitter herbs are blessed and eaten (horseradish/romaine lettuce)
10. *Korech*: *Matzah* is dipped in bitter herbs and eaten
11. *Shulchan Orech*: The meal is eaten (often lamb)
12. *Tzafun*: Children search for *afikomen*, everyone eats a small piece (dessert)
13. *Berach*: Grace after the meal, third cup of wine
14. *Hallel*: Praise, read Psalms, fourth cup of wine
15. *Nirtzah*: *Seder* is complete, accepted, give thanks

Step 1: *Kadesh*

This first cup of the Passover *seder* is called the Cup of Sanctification or *Kiddush* in Hebrew. As we sit around the *seder* table, we recite *Kiddush*, a special Hebrew blessing over the first cup (*Kos rishon*) of Passover wine or grape juice.

When we raise this cup and bless it, we remember that God not only separated us from the Egyptians but sanctified us to

Himself as a people. So when we recite the blessing, we are crying out to God to make us and this night holy!

Lord sanctify me. Make me Kadosh lecha—*holy unto you!*

Fill your cup with the first glass of wine or grape juice, lift the cup, say the *Kiddush*, and drink, leaning to the left. Tradition says to fill the cup to the brim, but it also says that you shouldn't get drunk, so you only have to drink half the glass (which may be small).

Every time we drink one of the four cups of the Passover, we do so while reclining and leaning to the left. It is also a custom in our house to never refill your own cup. Why? On Passover, we celebrate freedom. We are no longer slaves but royalty, and we eat and drink as such. We are children of the King. The *seder* is a divine drama that helps us embody and fully understand this spiritual truth. To celebrate our freedom and position as children of the King, we recline.

Step 2: *U'rchatz*
(handwashing with no blessing)

The second step is a ritual washing—a symbolic spiritual cleansing by pouring water over the hands. The water should be warm to make the washing pleasant. A pitcher of water is traditionally used to pour water over the right and then over the left hand. Afterward, you can dry your hands on a towel. In some homes and in a large congregation, the leader often acts as a proxy, performing the *u'rchatz* for the attendants. Ordinarily, a blessing is spoken over the ritual washing of the hands, but not this time. Usually, we only wash before we eat bread. Why do we wash at this point? It is to raise the awareness of the children, to get them to ask the question:

Why is this night different from all other nights?

Much of the *seder* is designed to engage the kids. **Exodus 13:8:** "You are to tell your son on that day saying, 'It is because of what ADONAI did for me when I came out of Egypt.'"

Step 3: *Karpas*
(eating the green vegetable)
The first bite of food people eat is the *karpas*, the green vegetable symbolizing spring and renewal. Parsley is often used and represents the hyssop that the Israelites used to apply the blood of the Passover lamb to the doorposts and lintel of their houses. Before eating the *karpas*, you dip it in saltwater, which stands for the tears of slavery and the sweat of hard labor. Other than its ritual symbolism, *karpas* serves as an *hors d'oeuvres* before the meal. *Karpas* acts as an appetizer that cleanses the palate, preparing for the other food that follows.

Step 4: *Yachatz*
Yachatz ("divide") is the fourth step of the *seder*. Before the *seder* begins, three pieces of *matzah* are placed in a three-tiered pouch (called a *matzah tosh*). The *seder* leader takes

the middle piece of *matzah* and breaks it into two uneven pieces. The smaller piece is placed back in the *matzah tosh*/bag. The larger piece is wrapped up in white linen cloth and is hidden as the kids cover their eyes. The kids will search for it after the meal, and whoever finds it will get a reward. This middle piece of hidden *matzah* is known as the *afikoman* (dessert). The broken *matzah* is then lifted for all to see as the head of the household recites:

This is the lechem oni—*the bread of affliction—that our forefathers ate in the land of Egypt.*

Why three pieces of *matzah*? Three is one of the most foundational numbers in Jewish thought. There are three patriarchs of Israel—Abraham, Isaac, and Jacob. The people of Israel are divided into three groups—priests, Levites, and the rest of the people.

Why is the middle piece broken into two parts? The middle piece relates to Isaac, the second patriarch, who was bound upon the altar at Moriah, where the temple would ultimately be built (Gen. 22). The sacrifice of Isaac foreshadowed and pointed to the death of another Son—the Messiah, the Son of God. The two parts refer to the two aspects of the Messiah: Son of Joseph (the suffering Son) and Son of David (the victorious Son). Also, the two parts refer to the two redemptions by the Messiah—He redeems Israel and the nations. In Jewish thought, the world is also broken up into two times: *Olam Hazeh* (this world) and *Olam Haba* (the world to come). It makes sense why one piece is smaller and the other is bigger. This temporal world is a blip on the radar screen of eternity in comparison to the eternal world, which is endless. This first, smaller piece is the bread of affliction—the poor man's bread. The poverty/slave mentality is no longer ours in the eternal world nor in the temporal world when we have the renewed mind of the Messiah. Passover is the physical, mental, and emotional liberation from slavery in this world. In the world to come, God will turn our mourning into dancing and wipe every tear from our eyes in the world to come.

Step 5: *Maggid*

Usually the longest of the fifteen *seder* steps, the *Maggid* is the retelling of the Exodus narrative. The youngest child at the table typically asks the four questions (every *haggadah* lists them). However, any person can read the questions, or everyone can read them together. The four questions all revolve around the fundamental question "Why is this night different from all other nights?" (*Mah nishtanah halailah hazeh mikol haleilot?*) The rest of the *Maggid* answers this question with the story of the Hebrews' exodus from Egypt, some *Torah* study, and a discussion of the description of the four types of children—the wise child, the wicked child, the simple child, and the child who doesn't know enough to ask a question.

We begin the retelling of the Passover story with the following declaration:

This is the lechem oni—the bread of affliction—that our forefathers ate in the land of Egypt. Whoever is hungry, let them come and eat. All who are needy, let them come and celebrate the Passover with us.

The *Maggid* fully displays the power of testimony. It also focuses on the power of words. While reading the book of Exodus, one might wonder at the swift descent of the Hebrew nation from being the privileged family of the viceroy, Joseph, to becoming downtrodden and abused slaves. Xenophobia, the fear of foreigners, is a common historical phenomenon. But one would think that transforming a nation into slaves would take generations or result in rebellion. The sages, however, explain in the *Midrash* that the Egyptians were cunning and enslaved the people of Israel through artifice.

This trickery is understood from Pharaoh, whose name can be broken up to mean *peh rah,* which means "evil speech" and can be understood as well to relate to *peh rach,* "soft speech."

Proverbs 18:21 says, "The tongue has the power of life and death" (NIV). Language is a powerful tool, and even Pharaoh understood this. When he decided to enslave the people of Israel, he declared a national week of labor. During this week, all good citizens of the realm were to come and help in the building of the great cities of Pithom and Ramses, with Pharaoh himself in the lead. The Israelites, wanting to show their considerable loyalty to their host country, joined in enthusiastically. The next day, however, when the people of Israel arrived at the building sites, the Egyptians did not return. Shortly after that, the Israelites found themselves surrounded by task-masters who demanded that they perform the same amount of work that they had done of their own volition the day before. It was through soft and cunning words that Pharaoh lured the Hebrew nation into slavery.

Not only is this *Midrash* interesting, but it is reflective of the importance that Jewish thought *and* Jewish law place on the use of words. So crucial is the impact of words to the Jews that Jewish law even forbids the use of words to manipulate another person into paying for lunch (let alone to enslave them).

Finally comes the pouring of the second cup of wine, but don't drink it yet. Traditionally, you dip a finger into the wine and transfer ten drops of wine to your plate, one for each of the ten plagues in Egypt. Then, after songs praising God and pointing out the various items on the *seder* table yet again, recite the blessing over the wine and drink of the second cup.

Step 6: *Rachtzah*
(handwashing with a blessing)

It's time to rewash your hands, but this time you *do* say the blessing. It's customary not to speak at all between washing your hands and saying the blessings over the *matzah*. You can use this time to reflect on the sanctification and purification that you're undergoing. In the temple, the priests had to serve and eat in a state of spiritual purity.

Just as the priests washed, so observant Jews wash their hands before eating bread. For eating is a holy act. Spirituality and food go hand in hand. Sin came through food. Yeshua-Jesus often met with people over meals because food and fellowship go together.

The blessing is called *Netilat Yadaayim*, which means not to wash but to lift up.

Eating is meant to be a spiritual act. The washing of our hands does not involve soap because it is also symbolic and spiritual, indicating sanctification and purification.

1. Wash the right hand three times, then the left three times.
2. Hold the handles of the cup with a towel.
3. Leave some water in the left hand; rub hands together.
4. Say the blessing.
5. *Matzah* (eating the *matzah*)

Blessings are said, and everyone breaks off a piece of *matzah* and eats it.

Step 7: *Motzi*
(blessing of the unleavened bread)

Matzah is the most important item in the *Seder*. The next two steps involve this unique unleavened bread. One blessing many Jewish people use in this step is "Blessed be You, Lord our God, King of the World, who brings bread out of the earth."

The Israelites were literally buried in Egypt and nearly lost their identity. But God delivered them out of slavery. He brought freedom from oppression as a seed of wheat, buried in the ground, bursts forth, comes alive, and grows.

Step 8: *Matzah*

(eating of the *matzah*)

The eating of the *matzah* is mentioned in step 6. But there's more. The Passover lamb was eaten on the first night, but *matzah* was eaten for the seven days of the festival. No leavened bread or products are eaten during Passover week.

There is a twofold reason that Jews eat *matzah*. The first is that after the tenth plague, the Egyptians drove the children of Israel out of Egypt quickly because they feared more Egyptians would die. The Israelites had to leave so hastily that their bread did not have time to rise (leaven). This is why the Lord told them, "You are to eat [the Passover] this way: with your loins girded, your shoes on your feet and your staff in your hand. You are to eat it in haste" (Ex. 12:11).

The second reason is that the *matzah* reminds Jews of the affliction their ancestors endured as slaves. Even its physical characteristics are reminiscent of oppression, such as the brown stripes running the length of the bread that point to the lashings of the slave drivers upon the enslaved Hebrews.

Matzah is also known as the bread of "freedom and healing" and serves as a reminder of when God redeemed Israel from Egypt "with an outstretched arm" (Ex. 6:6). The *matzah* is pierced, striped, bruised, and broken at the *seder*. It is meant to point prophetically to the Messiah promised in Isaiah 53.

During the Last *Seder*, *matzah* was the bread Yeshua lifted, broke, and "gave to the disciples and said, 'Take, eat; this is My body'" (Matt. 26:26). The *matzah*'s holes stand for His piercings, and the brown stripes represent His wounds, by which we are healed and set free from bondage to sin. His body was broken in death, like the *matzah*, so that the power of death might be broken and we might find eternal life.

Step 9: *Maror*
(eating the bitter herb)

Whether you eat a fresh slice of horseradish (known as Jewish Dristan) or a leaf of romaine lettuce (which is pretty wimpy), you should be thinking of the bitterness of slavery. Traditionally, you should dip the *maror* in the *charoset* (the apple-nut-wine-cinnamon mixture that represents the mortar used for the bricks) to taste a small amount of sweetness along with the pain.

On the night Yeshua was betrayed, John 13:26–27 shows, He revealed His betrayer: "'It is the one to whom I will give this piece of bread when I have dipped it in the dish.' Then, dipping the piece of bread, he gave it to Judas, the son of Simon Iscariot. As soon as Judas took the bread, Satan entered into him" (NIV). In addition to the bitterness of slavery, this step of dipping represents the bitterness of separation from Yeshua as exemplified by Judas.

Step 10: *Korech*
(Hillel's sandwich)

While the English Earl of Sandwich is generally given credit for inventing the snack of his namesake, Hillel, a Jewish religious leader circa 110 BC, may have originated it by combining *matzah*, a slice of the paschal lamb, and a bitter herb. Jews no longer sacrifice and eat the lamb, so the Passover sandwich is only *matzah*, *charoset*, and *maror* (many people use the *chazeret* instead of horseradish).

Step 11: *Shulchan Orech*
(eating the meal)

After eating the *korech*, it's time for the real meal. The main meal usually begins with a hard-boiled egg dipped in saltwater and quickly progresses to *gefilte* fish with horseradish, *matzah*-ball soup, chopped liver, and as much other food as you want to serve.

Although you drink four ceremonial glasses of wine during Passover, this doesn't preclude you from having some more during dinner if you so desire. This feast also symbolizes the wedding banquet of the messianic age the apostle John speaks of in Revelation 19:9: "Blessed are those who are invited to the wedding supper of the Lamb!" (NIV).

Step 12: *Tzafun*
(eating the *afikomen*)

Whether or not there's room for dessert after dinner, the last food that is officially eaten at the *seder* is a piece of the *afikomen matzah* (see step 4), which symbolizes the *Pesach* sacrifice. If the *afikomen* is hidden or stolen by the children, it must be returned or redeemed by the children and given to the leader by the *seder*'s end. The *seder* must end before midnight, according to tradition, and can't be completed without the *afikomen*. The children are usually tired at this point, so both sides have strong bargaining positions. Any taste of *matzah* will do once the *afikomen* has been returned.

The *afikomen* also represents the part of the self/soul that is lost or given up in slavery. The *seder* symbolizes the journey from enslavement to freedom. At *Tzafun*, people reclaim the pieces of self they were missing. Again, it's traditional to ingest the representation to internalize it.

Amazingly, *afikomen* is one of maybe two Greek words (the common language of Yeshua-Jesus' day) in the Passover *seder*. Everything else is in Hebrew. The translation is astounding. The word can mean "I have come." The *matzah*, with its stripes and piercings, is the most messianic of symbols. The *afikomen* takes it one step further as it is wrapped in a white linen cloth and hidden, just as Yeshua's body was pierced and wrapped in linen and buried in the tomb. The *afikomen* found at the end of the meal symbolizes how the women found Yeshua-Jesus the morning He rose. Partaking of the *afikomen* represents our partaking of His resurrection. Redeeming the *afikomen* stands for His redemption of us. This part of the *seder* has so many messianic overtones that possibly the traditional Jewish community received this ritual from the first-century messianic community.

Step 13: *Barech*
(blessing after eating)
Jewish meals always end with a blessing, and this meal is no exception. At this point, however, the meal may be completed, but the *seder* is not. The third cup of wine celebrating the meal is poured and drunk after reciting a blessing. This third cup is

known as the Cup of Redemption. It was this third cup that Yeshua raised at the Last Supper as Luke 22:20 tells us: "In the same way, He took the cup after the meal, saying, 'This cup is the new covenant in My blood, which is poured out for you.'"

Then, a seemingly curious tradition occurs: a cup of wine is poured in honor of the prophet Elijah, and a door is opened to allow Elijah to enter. One custom invites each person to pour a little of their wine to fill Elijah's cup. This pouring symbolizes each person's own responsibility and contribution toward bringing about redemption, which is when Elijah returns. According to Malachi 4:5–6 (3:23–24 in the Tree of Life Version), Elijah will return to prepare the way for the Messiah. This verse reflects the messianic expectation of the return of Yeshua-Jesus. These verses are also the last verses of the Old Testament in Christian Bibles.

Step 14: *Hallel*
(songs of praise)
After closing the door, the final *seder* ritual includes singing festive songs of praise to God and then filling, blessing, and drinking the fourth and final cup of wine. The songs of praise are from Psalms 113–118. After we experience the redemption of God, all we can do is thank Him and praise Him. As a paraphrase of Psalm 118:14–15 reminds us, "ADONAI is my strength and song, and He has become my salvation." Psalm 118:22 goes on to say, "The stone the builders rejected has become the capstone." This psalm is the most quoted messianic psalm of the New Testament. It is also the exact center of the Bible.

Step 15: *Nirtzah*

(conclusion)

The prescribed rituals and actions conclude at the fourteenth step; *Nirtzah* celebrates this conclusion. The most common prayer at the end is simply *L'shana haba-a bi-Y'rushalayim*, meaning "Next year in Jerusalem!"

The *seder* has relatively clear rules and an established procedure or order, but what makes the evening uncommon are the extra flourishes and different touches that all the participants add along the way. You have plenty of room to be creative and add to the *seder*—additional songs, prayers, poems, stories, commentary, and so on. If you aren't having fun, you aren't doing it right.

Shavuot/Pentecost is the culmination of Passover and Firstfruits. Pentecost found the people physically, emotionally, and spiritually freed. This freedom allowed them to enjoy the outpouring of His Spirit and understand and respond to the bountiful harvest of His Word.

CHAPTER THREE

THE STORY OF *Shavuot* PENTECOST

From the day after the Sabbath, the day you
brought the sheaf of the wave offering,
count off seven full weeks. Count off fifty days
up to the day after the seventh Sabbath,
and then present an offering of new grain to
the LORD. . . . I am the LORD your God.
Leviticus 23:15–17, 22 NIV

The Promise of Pentecost—Revelation of Word and Spirit . . .

As a child, do you remember the mounting excitement you felt when your birthday was approaching? I still relive it as I watch my kids with their countdown calendars. They start at about thirty days and tick off time as each day passes. They can't wait for the party, the balloons, the cake, and the presents. The anticipation is almost more than they can handle as the day gets closer.

You can think of this next holiday in much the same way. *Shavuot*, also known as Pentecost, is a celebration, and God rejoices if we brim with the anticipation of a child nearing his or her birthday. But unlike any other party, Pentecost is topped off with the giving of the greatest gift possible—God's Word and the Holy Spirit. In the Old Testament, God presented the gift on Mount Sinai in the form of the *Torah* (the first five books of the Old Testament). In the New Testament, the gift was presented by the infilling of the Holy Spirit in Acts 2.

THE COUNTDOWN

Now, this can get a bit tricky, but buckle up and hang on.

Jesus died on Passover. On the second day of Passover, He arose on the holiday called Firstfruits (*Yom Habikkurim*), which was an agricultural holiday. In ancient times, a firstfruits offering from the barley harvest was given to the Lord, which was the wave offering referred to in the Leviticus excerpt above. It would be waved before the Lord as a sign of thanksgiving and also in eager expectation. If you had an abundant early harvest, it was a guarantee that you would also have an abundant later harvest. Not only was the firstfruits a sign of the greater harvest to come, but it started the forty-nine-day countdown to *Shavuot*/Pentecost.

We have always acknowledged that nothing is random with God. Therefore, it is appropriate that Jesus, who died on Passover, would rise from the dead as "the firstfruits of those who have fallen asleep" (1 Cor. 15:20 NIV). After He rose, He instructed the disciples, "Do not leave Jerusalem, but wait for the gift my Father promised . . . For John baptized with water, but in a few days you will be baptized with the Holy Spirit" (Acts 1:4–5 NIV). His resurrection on Firstfruits started the countdown to Pentecost, which was His Father's gift—the biggest biblical celebration on record. Pentecost is when God rocked the house, and there were three thousand people saved in one day (Acts 2:41)!

Now, let's take a step back into the Old Testament and explore the first Pentecost on Mount Sinai.

THE PREPARATION

Earlier, I drew an analogy to a birthday because everyone can relate to that—we all have birthdays. However, the preparation of God's people for the first Pentecost was more comparable to a wedding. Like a bridegroom, God had to woo them. He had to win back the hearts and trust of a people who had been physically, emotionally, and spiritually ravaged by centuries of slavery. He had to demonstrate His love.

THE ROMANCING OF THE CREATED BY THE CREATOR

Some grooms make a big show when they ask for the bride's hand. They hire a skywriter to pop the question across the blue expanse, or they use the Jumbotron at a Dodger game to do the talking for them. God wanted to get the attention of His beloved in a big way as well.

At the first Passover, the angel of death slew the firstborn son of each Egyptian household. In contrast, the firstborn of the Hebrew households that applied lamb's blood to their doorposts were saved. Because of this, in Jewish thought, the firstborn son always belongs to the Lord. Then God made a big splash, literally, by parting the Red Sea and allowing them to walk across on dry land while the sea swallowed their pursuers. *Manna* fell from the sky, and stones flowed with water. The weather never wore out their clothes or shoes; a glory cloud by day sheltered them from the relentless sun, and a column of fire at night lit their way. The poet Elizabeth Barrett Browning asked, "How do I love thee? Let me count the ways." The Creator of the universe made a lavish display of His love in numerous ways to His beloved. In a sense, God had to prove *Himself* to them. Why?

FOUR HUNDRED YEARS UNDONE IN FIFTY DAYS

For generations, the people of Israel had been the beasts of burden, if you will, of the Egyptians. To the Egyptians, they were objects, not people. Century upon century passed; prayers, supplications, desperate cries rose from their souls to seemingly deaf heaven. They felt forgotten. God warned Abraham in Genesis 15 that four hundred years of affliction would befall the Jews, but who knows why four centuries had to pass before God moved? It's a question I have for Him once I'm on the other side. However, we know that God is never in a hurry, and He is also never late. Because of this protracted captivity, He needed to win back their trust and their love. He had to rebuild a relationship. See, God had a big gift in store for His people. However, for them to receive it properly, they needed to be healed and prepared, or the gift would have no meaning, and the purpose would be lost.

Just as we can question why it took God four hundred years to rescue Israel from Egypt (remember from the Passover chapter that the number four and multiples of the number represent exile and redemption), we can also ask why He waited *fifty* days from the time they escaped Pharaoh to the giving of the Ten Commandments on Sinai. Why not 40 days or 60 days or 365 days?

The number fifty stands for freedom. Biblically, the fiftieth year is the Year of Jubilee, in which all slaves return to their families and land returns to its original owner. All debt is canceled. Fitting, isn't it? The number fifty in Hebrew is also associated with wisdom. In Jewish thought, a person does not reach wisdom before fifty years of age.

Additionally, the numerical value of the Hebrew word for *water* equals the number fifty. The Talmud explains that water symbolizes *Torah*. As water sustains the body, *Torah* sustains the soul. The gift that awaited God's people for which they needed preparation was the spiritual water of the *Torah*. But, before they could drink of its depths and have their thirst quenched, they needed to be healed and whole. God worked His wonders within fifty days of redeeming them from Egypt.

HOLY AND WHOLE

Physical displacement has spiritual components, as we mentioned in the previous chapter. God took Israel out of Egypt. Now, He had to take Egypt out of Israel. Their enslavement in Egypt left the people scarred relationally, emotionally, psychologically, physically, and spiritually. They were in dire need of healing. They needed to rebuild a relationship not only with God but also with each other. The centuries of abuse in Egypt had slimed the people of Israel on all levels.

One of the key things that God needed to cleanse Israel of was their *sinat hinon*, their senseless hatred for one another that led to disunity. He had to break their slave mentality. Recall the incident of the two Hebrew slaves who Moses found fighting with one another. While trying to put an end to their dispute, they said to Moses, "Will you kill us like you killed the Egyptian taskmaster?" (see Ex. 2:14). Violence, oppression, and hatred were all that they knew. They had learned to deal with one another the way the Egyptians dealt with them—with verbal, mental, and physical abuse. This method was in extraordinary contrast to how ancient Hebrew justice worked. Justice was not about enslavement but about rehabilitating with dignity. Slavery was a punishment for a crime, frequently unpaid debt. However, slaves were not treated as chattel but as part of the family. For instance, if there were two slices of bread left, and one was good and one was spoiled, the master would give the servant the good one. If a slave had a family of their own, the entire family would be provided for by the master. They never split apart families, and enslavement was never permanent. In the seventh year, slaves were allowed to be free. The idea was that being treated by the person in authority, their masters, with goodness and grace, was transformative. In diametric opposition, the Egyptian method was destructive.

The people of Israel were also spiritually impure. For centuries, their masters were idolaters. Everywhere was pagan worship. They spilled their sweat and blood in the building of monuments to man and idols. Paganism was their environment for generations, which eventually and sadly influenced them to create the golden calf once they were out of Egypt.

Physically, they were broken by not only the abuse of the taskmasters but also the ruthless, relentless severity of the work. The enslaved Israelites had broken bodies, minds, hearts, and spirits. It's almost hard to fathom that this multidimensional healing and undoing of four centuries of horror could happen in only fifty days. Two verses come to my mind: "Nothing will be impossible with God" (Luke 1:37) and "Hope deferred makes the heart sick, but longing fulfilled is a tree of life" (Prov. 13:12). God wanted them to grab hold of this tree, whose roots were deep and unshakable in the fertile soil of His salvation. He breathed new life into His people by His deliverance of them from Egypt, His extravagant display of love through signs and wonders, His bountiful provision in the barren desert, and His healing of their bodies. He wanted them whole in order to be able to bestow upon them the gift of His holiness, His presence.

God wanted them expectant, prepared, and excited about what was coming. He had the heart of not only a Father but also a groom toward His bride, for Israel at this point was not only His beloved but His betrothed.

THE MARRIAGE ON MOUNT SINAI

*[ADONAI said to Moses,]"Be ready for the third day. For on the third day ADONAI will come down upon Mount Sinai in the sight of all the people. . . . **All** the people witnessed the thundering and the lightning, and the sound of the shofar, and the mountain smoking. When the people saw it, they trembled and stood far off."*
Exodus 19:11; 20:18

First, I want you to notice the word "all." There were millions of people rescued from Pharaoh. Given the various ages of the people and the inevitable number of broken bodies due to their daily toil, you can imagine the amount of infirm among them. However, God healed them ALL, for who wants a broken bride? *All* were able to come to the mountain. All could stand, all could hear, all could see His natural spectacles—thunder, lightning, fire, glory clouds. Just like a groom makes a covenant with his bride, God made covenant with His bride, Israel, in giving her the gift of His Word, the *Torah*, to instruct and guide her so that her heart remained His. He spoke the Ten Commandments (His Word) as His Spirit swirled about them in a lavish outpouring of His love and power.

The two tablets engraved with the commandments bear comparison to the *ketubah*—the wedding contract a groom gives to the bride. The couple displays the *ketubah* in their household as a constant, public reminder of their promise to one another. The clouds of glory were canopied overhead like the *chuppa*—the wedding canopy under which Jewish people are married. Moses was the matchmaker and best man (John 3:29). The analogies are endless. It is no wonder that Mount Sinai, in Jewish thought, correlates to a wedding.

A bride and groom go through a *mikvah*—a ritual bath that symbolizes they are purified and the sins of their previous lives before their marriage are wiped clean. They enter into this covenant of marriage in a state of spiritual purity and new beginnings. This spiritual purity is what God was doing for Israel as He instructed them to wash their clothes in preparation for the big day (Ex. 19:10). On that day, God Himself washed them in the water of His Word as if saying, "I have purified you, and now we have a fresh start and new beginning."

Shavuot/Pentecost is the culmination of Passover and Firstfruits. Passover physically freed the people; Firstfruits celebrated the promise of the harvest to come and thanked God for the provision at hand. Pentecost found the people physically, emotionally, and spiritually freed. This freedom allowed them to enjoy the outpouring of His Spirit and understand and respond to the bountiful harvest of His Word.

THE RELEVANCE OF *TORAH*

 At this point, I feel it is important to talk about why the *Torah* is still pertinent to followers of Yeshua. The *Torah* is synonymous with the Old Testament. Technically, the *Torah* is the five books of Moses. The entire Hebrew Bible, also known as the Old Testament, includes the *Torah*, the Writings, and the Prophets, which in Hebrew is known as the *TaNaK*.[1] The *Torah* was what Jesus would have read every week in the synagogue. The Old Testament was the Holy Scriptures of Jesus and the early church. In light of this significance alone, it's impossible to disregard it. The Old Testament is foundational to the New Testament, but frequently it is viewed as unnecessary in light of the New Covenant. However, this idea was never intended. I believe Jesus Himself clarifies this misconception in Luke 24, as mentioned in the preface.

Remember, grief weighed heavily on the followers of Jesus in the days following His death. Two of these men were on

---

1 The Jewish Virtual Library states, "[The word Tanakh] is derived from the Hebrew letters of its [Hebrew Scriptures] three components: Torah: The Books of Genesis, Exodus, Leviticus, Numbers, and Deuteronomy. Nevi'im (Prophets): The books of Joshua, Judges, 1 Samuel, 2 Samuel, 1 Kings, 2 Kings, Isaiah, Jeremiah, Ezekiel, Hosea, Joel, Amos, Obadiah, Jonah, Micah, Nahum, Habakkuk, Zephaniah, Haggai, Zechariah, and Malachi. Ketuvim (Writings): The books of Psalms, Proverbs, Job, Song of Songs, Ruth, Lamentations, Ecclesiastes, Esther, Daniel, Ezra and Nehemiah, 1 Chronicles and 2 Chronicles."

their way to Emmaus, recounting the previous day's horror and disappointment. A man (they didn't recognize Jesus) encountered them on the road. They explained the reason for their sadness. Jesus enlightened them by connecting the spiritual dots. He linked all the Old Testament prophecies to the Messiah and how the Messiah, the New Covenant, **fulfilled** them all, as stated in Matthew 5. He didn't negate the Old Testament. He joined the old to the new.

I am also reminded of what Jesus said in Matthew 13:52: "Therefore every teacher of the law who has become a disciple in the kingdom of heaven is like the owner of a house who brings out of his storeroom new treasures as well as old" (NIV). I believe the treasures that Jesus speaks of, old and new, are metaphors for the *Torah*/Old Testament *roots* and the New Covenant *shoots* as well as Jew and Gentile. Both are God's priceless possessions, neither one more or less valuable than the other. However, *together*, their value increases dramatically! When believers connect to the roots of their faith, more abundant fruits are the result—the revelation of our unity in Yeshua-Jesus. Christians are not obligated to keep all the *Torah*. But even though there is not *obligation* there is an *invitation* to learn and incorporate Old Testament teachings and events like the Jewish holidays into your life.

UNITED THEY STOOD

*And **all** the people answered together and said,*
"Everything that ADONAI *has spoken, we will do."*
Exodus 19:8

The word "all" in Exodus 19 tells us that every one of the Israelites was present on Mount Sinai to receive God's Presence. An interesting fact is that Jewish tradition states there are 600,000 letters in the *Torah*. Why is that something to note? Of all the people that exited Egypt, there were 600,000 men among them. The number of letters in the *Torah* match the number of men that left Egypt.

All signifies more than the obvious, however: "They travelled from Rephidim, came into to the wilderness of Sinai, and set up camp in the wilderness. Israel camped there, right in front of the mountain" (Ex. 19:2). In this passage, according to Rashi, a famous Jewish Bible commentator who lived in the Middle Ages, the people of Israel had finally reached a point of oneness, of **unity**. Rashi arrives at this conclusion based upon the fact the first time the word "camped" is used in this verse, it is written in the plural, but the second time it is used, it is in the singular. Rashi writes, "[They were] in a state of total unity, as if they were one person with one heart."[2] The experience of God's loving redemption created a *tikkun*, a correction, a transformation. The hostility of Egypt gave way to the unity of Sinai. Everything was purified, and in the process of purification came unification.

There are symbols of unity associated with Pentecost. Opposite to Passover, during which there is an avoidance of leaven, Pentecost/*Shavuot* is celebrated by presenting an offering of "two **loaves**" of "new grain to the LORD" (Lev. 23:16–17 NIV). You may wonder why leaven is allowable at Pentecost and

---

2 Chaim Miller, *Chumash: The Book of Exodus with Commentary from Classic Rabbinic Texts and the Lubaviticher Rebbe* (Brooklyn, NY: Kol Menachem, 2005–2009), 131.

forbidden at Passover. In Jewish thought, after we have purified ourselves of the leaven and what it represents, then that which is impure is transformed and sanctified by faith. This transformation makes the leaven no longer taboo.

Notice there's an offering of not one but **two** loaves. Two represents the unity between Word and Spirit, heaven and earth, body and soul, Jew and Gentile. *Shavuot* represents not only unity but the unification of opposites, which is why the book of Ruth is read during this holiday. There was power in the unlikely marriage between Boaz, the Israelite, and Ruth, the Gentile. From their union is the lineage of Yeshua. Jesus' final prayer in John 17 asks for unity among God's people just as He and the Father are one (John 17:21). The same language Rashi used to describe the love and unity that existed among Israel at Sinai is the same language used in the book of Acts to describe followers of Yeshua before, on, and after *Shavuot*.

These all continued with one accord in prayer and supplication, with the women and Mary the mother of Jesus, and with His brothers. (Acts 1:14 NKJV)

When the Day of Pentecost had fully come, they were all with one accord in one place. (Acts 2:1 NKJV)

And through the hands of the apostles many signs and wonders were done among the people. And they were all with one accord [one in heart] in Solomon's Porch. (Acts 5:12 NKJV)

Oneness! That is God's heart for His people, then and now. There's might in unity. The reason why armies march in step is due to the power of resonance.

When Roman armies marched in unison, bridges would break under them. Some experts speculate that if millions of people marched in step on the Golden Gate Bridge, the bridge would come down. That is the power of unity. Against all the odds and in record time, the people rebuilt the temple walls in Nehemiah's day because they were unified. God wouldn't give the gift of His Word and Spirit until **all** were present at Sinai, not just in head count but in their hearts. He wanted them *all* to be considered a royal nation, a royal priesthood. Only then would He release His presence. It was when they were in **one accord** in Jerusalem that the promised power came.

> Suddenly, there was a sound from heaven like the roaring of a mighty windstorm, and it filled the house where they were sitting. Then, what looked like flames or tongues of fire appeared and settled on each of them. And everyone present was filled with the Holy Spirit and began speaking in other languages, as the Holy Spirit gave them this ability. (Acts 2:2–4 NLT)

Acts 2 is meant to be a reenactment of Mount Sinai. The booming of the wind is like the thunderings at Sinai. The tongues of fire over the disciples' heads are a parallel to the cleft tongue that came out of the mouth of God when He uttered the commandments. According to the *Targum*, an ancient Aramaic paraphrase or interpretation of the Hebrew Bible, the split tongue looked like a fiery bird, which is said to have inscribed the tablets of the covenant. It reads, "Like torches of fire, a torch of fire to the right and a torch of fire to the left. It flew and winged swiftly in the air of the heavens and came back . . . and returning it became engraved on the tablets of the covenant and all Israel beheld it."[3]

In Acts 2, God again imprinted His Word as He did on Sinai. This time, God did not write His commandments on stone tablets like at Sinai but instead wrote His New Covenant *within* them on the tablets of their hearts: "I will make a new covenant with the house of Israel . . . I will put My *Torah* [Law] within them [in their minds]. Yes, I will write it on their heart" (Jer. 31:30, 32).

This unity of God's people, first on Sinai, then many years later in Jerusalem, sparked the fire and wind of the Spirit, which then created a wildfire of transformation. I hold firmly to the fact that God's **presence**, **power**, and **provision** are in direct proportion to the unity of His people.

REDEMPTION AND REVELATION

At this point, I need to shine a light on a truth that we cannot overlook. God physically redeemed Israel from Egypt and emotionally and spiritually redeemed them as well to make them a whole, holy nation. We must realize that as He was preparing them for redemption, He was also readying them for revelation. Here's an important truth: redemption without revelation can slide into reverse, regressing us to that place from which we

---

3 Targum Neofiti 19:2, The Aramaic Bible, Translated by Martin McNamara.

were redeemed (our own Egypt and its bondage). The purpose of redemption *IS* revelation. It's how God wanted them to live. It's why God freed them. Without a new purpose, a renewed mindset, a fresh identity, we can easily slip into slavery to Pharaoh again. Egypt can take many forms—our careers, our bank accounts, even our families. We are redeemed, set free, absolved, saved so that the revelation of who we are in God's divine plan can be made known to us and, more than made known, *understood*! It's not enough to be redeemed. We need the revelation of God's Word to fully understand how He wants us to live and be—free to serve God and not do what our ego-filled selves want to do. Complete transformation comes from redemption and revelation. With Pentecost came revelation.

Israel stood at Mount Sinai, and God gave them a new identity. They were no longer slaves to idolaters but a royal priesthood of the Most High. In the book of Acts, the disciples were no longer waiting in the wings but boldly stepping out center stage to a vast crowd, drawn by the spectacle of the Spirit, as apostles of the Gospel of peace *and* power. When the *Ruach*, the Holy Spirit, fell on them, the disciples/apostles spoke in different tongues. Fifteen different languages. Why? Jewish pilgrims from many nations were gathered together in Jerusalem to celebrate *Shavuot*. Therefore, the testimony of Jesus was heard in their native tongues though they were many miles from home. The multiple languages spoken are again like Sinai, where Jewish tradition teaches that when God spoke the *Torah*, they heard seventy languages simultaneously. In fact, because of this, *Shavuot/Pentecost* is looked upon as the reversal of Babel.

At Babel, the building of a monument to themselves unified the people. Knowing the heart of man, God scrambled their languages so that they would disband. However, when man gathers for advancing Kingdom purposes, the opposite effect takes place: acceleration and advancement. Recall that Nehemiah and the people built the temple wall in a record fifty-two days. If everyone had worked for themselves and not in unison and didn't join together their pieces of the wall, it would have been a disjointed monument only to themselves and without any purpose.

A NEW CREATION

As God redeemed Israel, He has redeemed us through the Messiah. We, too, are a new creation with a new identity and purpose. Israel was called a royal priesthood, a holy nation, on Mount Sinai. Peter declares the same for *us* in the passage below:

But you are a chosen people, a royal priesthood, a holy nation, a people for God's own possession, so that you may proclaim the praises of the One who called you out of darkness into His marvelous light. Once were "not a people," but now you are "God's people." (1 Peter 2:9–10)

Peter became a new creation during Pentecost. Instead of the coward who denied Yeshua-Jesus three times, he became *Petra* (Peter), living up to the name Yeshua gave him, which in Greek means "rock." Peter, filled with the power of *Ruach*, preach his first sermon and birthed the early church during this Pentecost. Just as in Genesis, as the Spirit hovered over the deep, God spoke the Word, and creation occurred. As it was in the beginning, so it was on that *Shavuot* in Jerusalem—the union of Word and Spirit swelled the ranks of the followers of Yeshua by three thousand new *creations* that day. Word and Spirit result in newness of life.

What I love about *Shavuot* is that it reminds us to be radical people of both the Spirit and the Word. For the first time, Peter was imbued with the Spirit and moved in apostolic authority. Signs and wonders followed the apostles, and churches spread like wildfire (Acts 2:41–47). That is the Gospel of power.

Remember, what God has done in the past He wants to do again in the present and the future. The past is more than events that have already happened. They are a reflection of the desires of His constant, unwavering heart. He wants to wash you clean and take you as His beloved. Step away from the past and start a new future as His bride. During the Last Supper, when Jesus gave us communion through the bread and wine, He called the cup of wine the cup of the New Covenant (see 1 Cor. 11:25). The cup, in part, symbolized the ancient Jewish wedding tradition of the groom pouring out his life for his wife. Yeshua-Jesus poured out His life and made a New Covenant with us, His bride. We are a new creation, and just like ancient Israel, we are made whole and holy by the blood of the Lamb.

APOSTOLIC POWER:
PRESSING IN FOR ANOTHER PENTECOST

In addition to our new identity and purpose, which cements our unity as *His own special people,* a **hunger** for God sparks the outpouring of His presence. Look back at Acts 1:14. It states that Jesus' disciples were with "one mind . . . continuing together in prayer." As they met in the upper room for ten days, they were in harmony with each other. There were no arguments, no divided interests. Their deep grief and sense of loss led them to the throne of grace. Their only agenda was to pray and wait on God. Psalm 62:2 reminds us, "My soul, wait in stillness, only for God—from Him comes my salvation." Andrew Murray wrote,

> All that the church and its members need for the manifestation of the mighty power of God in the word is the return to our true place, the place that belongs to us, both in creation and redemption, the place of absolute and unceasing dependence on God.[4]

The disciples felt an outpouring of His presence as they waited and prayed.

An incredibly touching story always comes to mind:

> [There was a] blind girl, whose hard work had blunted her fingers, so that she could no longer read her Bible.

---

4 Andrew Murray, *Waiting On God* (Chicago, IL: Moody Publishers, 1958), eBook edition.

Her Bible was her most precious companion, her dearest friend, and the voice of God to her soul; how could she lay aside her Bible? She took a pen-knife, pared away the thick skin, and read again; but now she could not work. What is she to do? She *must* work: there is, therefore, no alternative, she must keep her blunt fingers, and lay aside her Bible. In despair she took it up, saying to it, "Dearly as I love thee, we must part," and putting it to her lips, to give it a farewell kiss, she discovered to her unspeakable joy, that there was soul enough in her lips to read the precious book.[5]

Doesn't a story like this one make you ask the question, *How hungry am I? How much more of God do I want?* Friends, God is a gentleman. He won't give you more of Himself than what you ask for. As a new follower of Yeshua, I hungered to experience the God of the Bible. I wanted to operate in the supernatural, like the first-century followers of the Messiah. God delighted in this desire of my heart. One day, as I was sitting at a conference, I heard God's voice, and He urged me, "Don't settle for a form of godliness that lacks power!" From that day forward, I purposed to never compromise on God's instruction.

Do you want your words to be backed by Kingdom power as in the book of Acts? I want another Pentecost. Do you? Are you willing to wait and pray and see God work?

---

5 John Pulsford, *Quiet Hours* (London: James Nisbet & Co., 1857), 228–229, public domain.

I assure you, God is listening just as attentively now as a century ago, as two millennia ago. Remember, He is constant and unchanging—the same yesterday, today, and forever (Heb. 13:8). His eyes are searching, and His ears are attuned to the prayers of His people. Let us pray to experience another *Shavuot*/Pentecost.

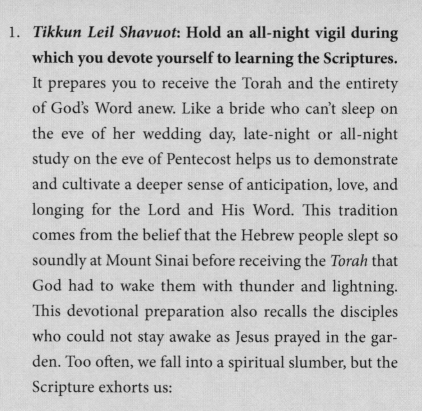

HOW TO CELEBRATE
Shavuot

1. *Tikkun Leil Shavuot*: **Hold an all-night vigil during which you devote yourself to learning the Scriptures.** It prepares you to receive the Torah and the entirety of God's Word anew. Like a bride who can't sleep on the eve of her wedding day, late-night or all-night study on the eve of Pentecost helps us to demonstrate and cultivate a deeper sense of anticipation, love, and longing for the Lord and His Word. This tradition comes from the belief that the Hebrew people slept so soundly at Mount Sinai before receiving the *Torah* that God had to wake them with thunder and lightning. This devotional preparation also recalls the disciples who could not stay awake as Jesus prayed in the garden. Too often, we fall into a spiritual slumber, but the Scripture exhorts us:

   > Awake, awake! Clothe yourself in your strength, Zion! Clothe yourself in beautiful garments. (Isa. 52:1)

> It is already the hour for you to awaken from
> sleep; for now our salvation is nearer than
> when we first came to trust. (Rom. 13:11)

Let's not be found sleeping but remain awake as we
eagerly await the return of the Messiah!

2. **On *Shavuot*, it is customary to eat two meals—one
   dairy, one meat.** The two meals represent the two loaves
   of bread that were brought to the temple as an offering
   on the first *Shavuot*. The first meal should be the dairy
   meal, and after a short break, we eat the meal of meat
   (or fish). We eat dairy because *Torah* is compared to milk
   as Scripture states in Song of Solomon 4:11—like honey
   and milk (*Torah*) lies under your tongue. Just like milk is
   the perfect food for sustaining children, milk is the key
   to nourishing the human soul (milk of the Word [1 Cor.
   3:2; Heb. 5:12]). The numerical value of the Hebrew word
   for milk, *chalav*, is forty. This connection commemorates
   the forty days Moses spent on Mount Sinai receiving the
   Torah. One customary dairy food we eat is cheesecake.
   The meat meal (7:26) signifies a feast—a celebration
   (food and drink were a way to delight yourself [Isa. 58]).
   For most people, this involves either meat or fish.

3. **Ornament your house with flowers and greenery.** This
   ornamentation represents Mount Sinai being dry and
   desolate until the giving of the *Torah*. At that point, it

became lush and green. Many Jewish people believe this is analogous to what God did with the modern State of Israel and fulfills His promise that He would make the desert bloom.

4. **Visit a synagogue to hear the reading of the Ten Commandments.** During *Shavuot*, all the Jewish people were able-bodied and healthy in order to gather at the foot of Mount Sinai to hear the Ten Commandments read and reaffirm their commitment to God and the *Torah*.

5. **Read the book of Ruth or go to a synagogue to hear it read.** *Shavuot* is the time of spring harvest (Ex. 23:16), and it is at this time that Ruth and Boaz met and fell in love. Secondly, King David, who is a direct descendant of Ruth and Boaz, was both born on *Shavuot* and died on *Shavuot*, according to Jewish tradition. It is significant that all this happens on *Shavuot*.

    Ruth was a Moabite, a people born out of the incestuous relationship between Lot and his morally and spiritually corrupt daughter. According to Jewish tradition, Ruth was a Moabite princess, so for King David, Israel's greatest king, to descend from her seems shocking. But Ruth's transformation from Moabite princess to a faithful believer and follower of the Lord mirrors Israel's process of being changed from slaves to sons and daughters of the covenant. Like Israel, they both started on a low level but were elevated into a place of new identity and destiny. Ruth, the Moabite, not only becomes part of the covenant people but is remembered for her role in birthing the line of David. The fact that Ruth is part of the line of David reminds us that it takes Jew and Gentile together to birth the Kingdom. For all these reasons, *Shavuot* celebrates not only the spring harvest and the giving of the *Torah* but also King David the warrior-*Torah* scholar and sweet singer-songwriter of Israel through whom the Messiah descends.

Israel had fallen to a very low place spiritually, morally, and economically as a result of generations of slavery. But the Passover began a fifty-day transformation process that culminated in *Shavuot*, the day God reaffirms His covenant with the children of Israel, gives them the *Torah* at Sinai, and bestows on them a new identity as "royal priesthood and a holy nation" (Ex. 19:6).

The Jewish New Year of *Rosh Hashanah* provides us with a clean slate, a fresh start, a do-over from anything in our lives that we feel is wasted or unworthy.

CHAPTER FOUR

Rosh Hashanah
YOM TERUAH (THE FEAST OF TRUMPETS)

The Lord said to Moses, "Give the following instructions to the people of Israel. On the first day of the appointed month in early autumn, you are to observe a day of complete rest. It will be an official day for holy assembly, a day commemorated with loud blasts of a trumpet. You must do no ordinary work on that day. Instead, you are to present special gifts to the Lord."

Leviticus 23:23–25

ROSH HASHANAH: A BRIEF OVERVIEW

Imagine the movie scene from the 1991 blockbuster hit *City Slickers.* Billy Crystal walks up and casually says, "Your life is a do-over. You've got a clean slate." Billy Crystal repeats this exact remark to a friend who is complaining about his wasted life. There is another famous movie line from *Anne of Green Gables* when Miss Stacy strengthens Anne with courage and hope: "Tomorrow is always fresh with no mistakes in it."

A clean slate. A fresh start. A do-over. They are all many names for the opportunity to start again. I remember being in third grade, playing kickball. I was big for my age and clumsy, but I was given grace in the form of many do-overs for which I was grateful. I remember how nice they felt.

The Jewish New Year of *Rosh Hashanah* is exactly that: a clean slate, a fresh start, a do-over from anything in our lives that we feel is wasted or unworthy. It is also a sealing for a good year. *Rosh Hashanah* is quite different from the American New Year, which is marked with football by day and beer bashing by night. *Rosh Hashanah* is remembered as a holy day, sanctified by day-long prayers for two days and characterized by honey-dipped apples, *challah* bread, and New Year's cheer. I remember getting all sticky with my buddies in Hebrew school from the honey, which represents a sweet new year. The stickiness symbolizes sticking to God and His sticking to us. The Hebrew word for this kind of bonding, *deveikut,* is the same word used in Genesis when describing a man *cleaving to* his wife. The round *challah* represents the fresh cycle of the new year ahead.

The *Torah* refers to this holiday as *Yom Ha-Zikkaron*, the day of remembrance, or *Yom Teruah*, the day of the sounding of the shofar. The blowing of the *shofar* is why this holiday is known as the Feast of Trumpets. Ancient Israel announced the coronation of a king by the blast of the *shofar*. By sounding the *shofar*, we, the crown of creation, recognize God as our Creator and King.

The primary spiritual action performed on this day is the blowing of the *shofar*, the ram's horn. Knowing the spiritual reasons why the *shofar* is sounded is key to both understanding the great spiritual significance of this holiday as well as experiencing its transformative power in our lives. Now let's explore the deeper meaning of this day and the meaning of the sound of the *shofar*.

THE SOUND OF THE *SHOFAR* IS A SPIRITUAL ALARM CLOCK

The sounding of the *shofar* ushers us into greater intimacy with God. God wants to encounter us. He created us for His pleasure and desire. He created us to love us. Yet, often in life, we lose our way, forgetting our true purpose—to love and be loved. The sound of the *shofar* is the sound of a spiritual alarm clock, as it is a call to return through *repentance*, which means to turn our wills and our ways to align with God's Word and will.

But repentance is more than feeling sorry, which can lead to conviction and remorse. True repentance is constructive, resulting in a real change in the way we think, ultimately leading to a change in our actions. Since none of us is perfect, we all fall short of God's best for our lives. Sin results in separation from God, each other, and also ourselves. It causes us to fall into a personal, self-inflicted exile from God, others, and self. The *shofar* blast is a call to turn from our transgressions and experience a better, deeper connection with God, self, and others. Sin is separation; repentance is reconnection.

The ten days between *Rosh Hashanah* and *Yom Kippur* are known as the Days of Awe and Repentance. There are two types of *teshuva* (repentance): repentance born out of fear of God and repentance born from love and awe of God. Fear-based repentance comes from an imperfect understanding of God. We view Him less as the lover of our souls and giver of grace, and more as one who doles out consequences and judgment.

Repentance motivated out of fear of retribution is not the best motivation for turning to God. Why? This type of repentance is more motivated by selfishness—it is the fear of punishment tainted with self-preservation. This fear should not be the driving motivation for us to repent and return to God. That is an imperfect form of *teshuvah*. The perfect form is known as *teshuvah mei'ahavah, repentance out of love*. It is turning from our transgressions and returning out of love because of an overwhelming sense of the awesomeness and grace of God. It is returning because we know that God loves us, desires us, and is relentlessly passionate for us. When we undeniably come to this revelation, we can't help but be transformed.

THE SOUND OF THE *SHOFAR* IS THE SOUND OF NEW BEGINNINGS AND BLESSINGS

Rosh Hashanah is a time of new beginnings and blessings. It was on the Feast of Trumpets that Sarah and Abraham conceived Isaac in their old age, according to Jewish tradition.[1] It was also on *Rosh Hashanah* that Rachel conceived Joseph[2] (and Hannah conceived Samuel after years of barrenness).

I believe the reason this day was chosen is that *Rosh Hashanah* has traditionally been understood as the birthday of creation. In Jewish thought, the sixth day of creation was the first day of the Hebrew month *Tishrei*. This means that the day God commands Israel to celebrate the Feast of Trumpets is the same day He created Adam and Eve. Thus, this day historically and spiritually is a time of life and blessing.

It for this reason that the primary spiritual act performed on *Rosh Hashanah* is the blowing of the *shofar*. You might be wondering, what is the connection? Think about it for a moment. What caused the first man to come to life? The blowing of the *shofar* reminds us of how God breathed the breath of life into Adam. Therefore, one of the reasons we blow the *shofar* to ring in the New Year is to celebrate the birthday of the world and, more specifically, the creation of humanity.

---

1 Babylonian Talmud. *Yevamot* 64b.
2 Babylonian Talmud. *Rosh HaShanah* 10b.

Spiritually, *Rosh Hashanah* is a time we go from barrenness to blessing. God wants you to have faith like Abraham and Sarah so you can conceive and receive His promised blessings for your life. In the same way the Lord breathed life into Adam, He wants to breathe new life into you and your destiny.

THE SOUND OF THE *SHOFAR* IS THE SOUND OF FREEDOM

Rosh Hashanah is also a day that God changes destinies. According to Jewish tradition, it was on *Rosh Hashanah* that Joseph was freed from prison in Egypt. His freedom came after being summoned to interpret Pharaoh's disturbing dreams. Joseph's skill of interpretation led to his ascent to becoming viceroy of Egypt, undoubtedly placing the Israelite community in a favorable position in the palace. It was on this date, centuries later, that the harsh labor of enslavement in Egypt ended for the people of Israel, planting the first seeds of the upcoming redemption, which culminated on Passover (B.T. *Rosh HaShanah* 10b–11a).

Spiritually, it makes sense that the Feast of Trumpets is the day the Lord chose for these two events to occur. Let me explain. The fall high holidays were when the captives were set free with the sound of the *shofar*. The *shofar* was sounded at the start of every seventh year, the sabbatical year—or in Hebrew, *Shimittah*—announcing that it was time to release all Hebrew slaves from their six years of indentured servitude. The sound of the *shofar* is the sound of freedom.

The start of the new year is the start of a new season in one's life. It therefore makes sense that Joseph and Israel began to experience freedom on this day. What God did for Joseph and the Israelites in Egypt He can do for you. From what pits and prisons do you need freedom? On *Rosh Hashanah*, you need to raise your voice like a *shofar* and cry out the Lord to set you free!

Every one of us has places of confinement and limitations in our lives, areas of slavery from which we need deliverance. The sound of the *shofar* reminds us that this is a time of freedom and destiny. No matter how long you have felt stuck and trapped, things can be different. The Lord can change your situation and circumstances like He did for Joseph in an instant. There is freedom in Yeshua! Be encouraged and remember that when "the Son sets you free, you will be free indeed!" (John 8:36).

THE SOUND OF THE *SHOFAR* IS THE SOUND OF CHANGE, TRANSFORMATION, AND HOPE

Rosh Hashanah is a time of change, transformation, and hope. In Hebrew, *Rosh* means "head," as in "beginning," and *Shanah* means "year." The word for *year* comes from the Hebrew word *shinui*, which means "changes." Thus, *Rosh Hashanah* is a time to experience change and transformation in our lives.

The sound of the *shofar* symbolizes that things can and will ultimately change. This promise of change should instill hope in our hearts, reminding us that our future will be better than our past. Ultimately, the *shofar* points us to the ultimate and blessed hope, the coming of the Messiah.

Prophetically, the first spring biblical festivals found in Leviticus 23 were fulfilled at Yeshua's first coming. He died as the Passover Lamb, rose from the dead on Firstfruits, and poured out the Holy Spirit on Pentecost, *Shavuot*. The fall holidays are awaiting their full prophetic fulfillment at the Second Coming. The Feast of Trumpets is meant to remind us of the final *shofar*, the trumpet of God, that will be sounded at the return of the Messiah:

> Behold, I tell you a mystery: We shall not all sleep, but we shall all be changed—in a moment, in the twinkling of an eye, at the last *shofar*. For the *shofar* will sound, and the dead will be raised incorruptible, and we will be changed. For this corruptible must put on incorruptibility, and this mortal must put on immortality. But when this corruptible will have put on incorruptibility and this mortal will have put on immortality, then shall come to pass the saying that is written: "Death is swallowed up in victory." (1 Cor. 15:51–54)

In the natural, the fall is a time when we experience a change in the seasons. The leaves change and the temperature drops. The same is true in the spiritual. The sound of the *shofar* is a call for change and transformation.

The *shofar* not only reminds us to live in light of the hope of the Messiah's return in which we will all be changed, but it also is meant to awaken hope in our hearts that we can be transformed right now, for in the Messiah we are "a new creation. The old things have passed away; behold, all things have become new" (2 Cor. 5:17). The New Year is meant to be a time of new beginnings, new breakthrough, and new blessing. You don't need to remain a slave to your old ways; the Lord wants to empower you by His Spirit to see and be different. In Yeshua, all things are made new, even you!

THE SOUND OF THE *SHOFAR* IS THE SOUND OF THE LORD'S PROMISE OF PROVISION

There are special Scripture readings on every biblical holiday. One of the primary readings on *Rosh Hashanah* is the binding of Isaac found in Genesis 22. In this passage, the Lord tests Abraham by commanding him, "Take your son, your only son whom you love—Isaac—and **go** to the land of Moriah, and offer him there as a burnt offering on one of the mountains about which I will tell you" (v. 2). Abraham and Isaac do go. Abraham binds Isaac upon the altar and is about to offer his beloved son to the Lord. At the last moment, an angel calls to Abraham and tells him not to sacrifice Isaac. Next, Abraham lifts up his eyes and sees a ram that was caught in the thicket by its horns. Abraham offers this ram in place of Isaac and then names that place "Adonai Yirah—as it is said today, 'On the mountain, Adonai will provide'" (v. 14).

One reason we read this story on *Rosh Hashanah* is that it involves a ram caught by its horns. The *shofar* (ram's horn) blown on the Feast of Trumpets reminds us that the Lord is our provider. Just like the Lord provided for Abraham and Isaac, we ask God to remember His covenant with us and provide for us as He did for our forefathers.

On *Rosh Hashanah*, the *shofar* is blown one hundred times. Abraham was born to Isaac when he was one hundred years old. From a Jewish perspective, Abraham is tested ten times, and ten squared is one hundred. The first test occurs in Genesis 12 when the Lord tells Abraham to leave everything and everyone behind to go a land that he will be shown. The last of the ten tests occurs in Genesis 22. In both these tests, the Lord uses the same Hebrew expression *Lech Lecha*, which means, "Go to yourself."

The command *Lech Lecha* has a numerical value of one hundred. Is this a coincidence? I think not. The first time the Lord commands Abraham to *Lech Lecha*, He is asking Abraham to trust Him with his past by leaving everything familiar. During Abraham's tenth and final test, when the Lord commanded Abraham for a second time to *Lech Lecha*, He was asking Abraham to trust Him to provide for his future. Isaac represented Abraham's future; for apart from him, there was no son to inherit or carry on the Lord's promise. The Lord asks each of us to do the same!

But of course, there is more. Many years later, Isaac, the son of promise, born when his father was one hundred years old, sowed in a year of famine. Because the Lord had blessed him, he reaped a hundredfold (Gen. 26:12). In the New Testament, Yeshua promises, "Everyone who has left houses or brothers or sisters or father or mother or children or property, for My name's sake, will receive a hundred times as much, and will inherit eternal life" (Matt. 19:29). Do you see the connection between the old and the new? All who are willing to leave everything for the Lord and trust the Lord will ultimately receive great blessing from the Lord like Abraham and Sarah.

On *Rosh Hashanah,* we must remember that God is our creator and provider. Do you have the faith that He can provide for you like He did for Abraham and Sarah? Are you willing to leave everything to trust and obey? If so, then, like Abraham, you will see God provide in powerful ways. I can attest to this in my own life and ministry.

Rosh Hashanah is a God-appointed time in which we need to pray for God's provision and blessing. **It is a traditional Jewish belief that God determines our financial provision for the coming year starting on** *Rosh Hashanah.*

But *Rosh Hashanah* is also a time to sow generously so that we might reap much like Isaac. We need to trust the Lord and commit to investing in the work of the Kingdom because *Rosh Hashanah* sets the foundation for the year. Are you willing to take a risk in what you sow even if it seems like a famine? Let me share a story with you to build your faith that this is possible.

I have a friend by the name of Tami who attends one of our several Fusion groups in California. She wanted to sow her tithe into our ministry (Fusion with Rabbi Jason) but felt that her tithe needed to go to her home congregation. But the Lord told her that she could give a sacrificial offering to our ministry.

Tami was confused because money was tight, and there usually was not anything extra in the budget to give. The Lord reminded her that she had an extra $1,000 coming from work.

This godly reminder did not make sense because she was planning to use $500 for her kids' back-to-school clothes and the other $500 for a down payment on braces for her daughter.

She prayed and sought counsel and felt that she needed to sow a $1,000 seed into our ministry. Tami felt that giving this gift was not only an act of faithfulness but would demonstrate to her children the power of God to provide. When Tami gave her gift online, this is what the Lord did. First, a friend came to her and said, "I feel like the Lord told me that I was to give you a $500 gift." Another person called and said the Lord wanted her to pay for her daughter's braces. She was shocked! Tami thought at first that the woman meant the down payment for the braces, but she was incorrect. The woman offered to pay the full bill of $5,000! But that's not all. Tami's work informed her that her hours had not been accurately calculated, and they owed her an additional $1,000!

Like Abraham and Sarah, Tami by faith took a big risk that would have had a huge impact on her kids. And in the end they were greatly blessed! The blessing always exceeds the sacrifice when you are faithful to God and are willing to invest in His Kingdom.

THE SOUND OF THE *SHOFAR* IS A CALL TO RETURN

Come, let us return to the LORD . . .
that we may live in his presence.
Hosea 6:1–2 NIV

The *shofar* is a call for God's people to arise, turn, and return to Him in greater relational intimacy. It's a return to our first love. On *Rosh Hashanah*, we remember God as Creator and King.

When we return to God, we experience transformation and restoration in our lives. By turning from sin and returning to the Lord, our relationship with God, self, and others is restored and heightened.

A necessary ingredient to restoration is our sense of awe. We have become a people desensitized by a plethora of modern means, including the media, and God wants to restore our awe. Think of the last time you stood in awe of something—a natural wonder, miraculous healing, the birth of a child. Remember how it felt? How beautiful, how unique a feeling it was? In a sense, the feeling was childlike. Jesus said in Luke 18 that we have to be like children to enter the Kingdom of God. This sense of awe is part of what He was talking about, I believe. One of my favorite memories involves a miracle of healing. I told this story earlier in the book, but I think it bears repeating because it reminds me of my sense of awe at the goodness of God each time I tell it.

One week after coming to faith, I received a phone call from Jeff, a homeless friend in NYC. He spent a cold winter's night in Chinatown on the streets. His legs had become frostbitten overnight, and he was hospitalized in NYU Medical Center, scared to death that he wouldn't walk again. What did I know? I had read the Gospels and the book of Acts. I thought, *We can do what they did.* Jeff was downcast and distraught. His legs were blackish and green. I said, "Jeff, I'm going to pray for you, and I believe that God can heal you." I laid hands on him and said, "Silver and gold have I none, but what I have, in the name of Yeshua, I say rise, take up your bed and walk." A couple of days later, Jeff walked out of the hospital with perfect legs.

Restoring a sense of awe of God is an essential priority. In ancient Israel, God was so revered and held in such esteem that His name was mentioned only *once* during the entire year—on the Day of Atonement (*Yom Kippur*). The high priest would enter the most sanctified of places, the Holy of Holies, and pronounce the actual name of God. Thinking on this, I can imagine the whispered, almost breathless, wonder that filled that sacred space at the mention of His name. Sadly, the Hebrew name for God has been lost over the centuries. Today, instead of reverence, God's name is often treated with disrespect and dismissal. People often don't consider His name as it rolls off our tongues in anger, fear, and rage and for shock value.

Remember what was written in the Ten Commandments in Exodus 20:7: "You shall not misuse the name of the LORD your God, for the LORD will not hold anyone guiltless who misuses his name" (NIV).

MINIMIZE THE CREATOR, MINIMIZE THE CREATED

The Hebrew word for taking the Lord's name in vain means to treat it as nothing. Can you imagine our regard for Him nose-diving from a place where His name was so holy it was said only once a year in the most sacrosanct of sites to be the careless expression of a range of our ugly emotions? When we diminish the Creator, we diminish the created as well. Man falls from the crown to the ground. There is no room for awe, only *awful*.

The books of Hebrews and Psalms remind us that He made us a little lower than Himself and higher than the angels. Think about this! When we are standing before an individual, we must have heaven's perspective and love each other with the same love that comes from the heart of the Father, which is what Paul is referring to when he encourages believers, "With humility consider others as more important than yourselves, looking out not only for your own interests but also for the interests of others" (Phil. 2:3–4). The next time you stand before a friend or a stranger, remember that a part of the Creator stands before us in His creation. I genuinely believe this will change how we interact with one another.

There is a famous rabbi named Abraham Joshua Heschel who spoke of the importance of awe and appreciation:

> Awe is more than an emotion; it is a way of understanding, an insight into a meaning greater than ourselves. The beginning of awe is wonder, and the beginning of wisdom is awe. Awe is an intuition for the dignity of all things, a realization that things not only are what they are, but also stand . . . for something supreme. Awe . . . enables us to perceive in the world intimations of the divine, to sense in small things the beginning of infinite significance.[3]

When we regard the Creator with awe, wonder, and respect, the work of His hands will be esteemed, for He is a part of it all. Our renewed and restored perspective will be like an

---

3 Abraham Joshua Heschel, *Who Is Man?* (Palo Alto, CA: Stanford University Press, 1965), 88.

expensive close-up lens, allowing us to see God's fingerprints in all things, from great and mighty things to even the smallest slivers of His goodness hidden in Creation. This sense of awe and wonder should cause us to revere the Lord and return to Him with all our hearts, minds, and strength. It should also create in us a deep sense of appreciation that such a great and awesome Creator and King loves and desires an intimate relationship with us.

GIVING AN ACCOUNTING OF OUR SOULS

Rosh Hashanah is also known as *Yom HaDin,* the day of judgment. Traditional Judaism holds that at the start of the New Year, the Lord examines every individual's life for blessing or judgment. The New Testament makes it clear that every one of us will stand before the Lord to give an account for our lives. Both believer and unbeliever alike will be judged for their actions as well as every word they speak:

> But I tell you that on the Day of Judgment, men will give account for every careless word they speak. For by your words you will be justified, and by your words you will be condemned. (Matt. 12:36–37)

> So whether at home or absent, we make it our aim to be pleasing to Him. For we must all appear before the judgment seat of Messiah, so that each one may receive what is due for the things he did while in the body— whether good or bad. (2 Cor. 5:9–10)

But you, why do you judge your brother? Or you too, why do you look down on your brother? For we all will stand before the judgment seat of God. (Rom. 14:10)

Behold, I am coming soon, and My reward is with Me, to pay back each one according to his deeds. (Rev. 22:12)

There is wisdom for all believers to learn to live with God's times and seasons. For followers of the Messiah who will have to stand before the Lord and answer for our lives, *Rosh Hashanah* is a time when we should examine our lives and turn from any sin or unpleasing actions for which the Spirit convicts. Rabbi Eliezer, a wise Jewish sage, said to his disciples, "Repent one day before your death." His disciples challenged him, saying, "But does anyone know the day of their death?" "All the more reason to repent today," replied Rabbi Eliezer. And as the author of Hebrews exhorts: "Today if you hear His voice, do not harden your hearts" (Heb. 3:15). Don't wait to examine your life. Turn from all wrongdoing, and return to the Lord with all your heart so that you might experience deeper connection and blessing from Him!

A RITUAL OF REPENTANCE AND RETURNING

A common practice on *Rosh Hashanah* is *tashlich*, which is translated as the "casting off." This tradition relates to Micah 7:19: "He will again have compassion on us. He will subdue our iniquities, and You will cast all our sins into the depths of the sea." On the afternoon of the first day of the high holidays, a congregation will walk to flowing water. At the banks of the river, they will empty their pockets, a symbolic picture of casting off their sins. Many bring small pieces of stale, old leavened bread to represent their sins. Why stale bread? We don't want to carry old leaven into the new year. Also, the fish will eat the bread bits and digest them, causing our symbolic sins to exist no more. I encourage you to find a body of water and do this either on your own or with your family and friends. It is such a powerful spiritual and prophetic act to throw your leaven/bread into the sea.

THE SOUND OF THE *SHOFAR* IS THE SOUND OF REGATHERING AND RESTORATION

I love this one very Jewish joke: A pastor travels to Rome and has an audience with the pope. He meets the pope and cannot help noticing the expensive phone on his desk, which is ornate with gold trim.

Surprised, the pastor asks, "What is that?"

The pope replies, "That is a telephone, and it is a direct line to heaven. Whenever I need a direct answer, I can pick it up and talk to God directly."

The pastor smiles, amazed, "Wow! Is it expensive?"

The pope answers, "Yeah, it is a long-distance call; it is about $100 a minute. It is a long way."

Then, the pastor continues his journeys and heads to Jerusalem. There, he enters the chief rabbi's office in Jerusalem. He discovers a phone on the desk that is engraved in a beautiful silver blue.

He says, "Rabbi, what is that phone? Actually, I believe that I know what it is."

The rabbi says, "Yeah, it is a direct line to heaven. Whenever I need to speak to heaven, I just pick up the phone."

The pastor smiles knowingly and comments, "Well, I was just in Rome, and it was very expensive."

The rabbi replies, "Really? How much is it? Here it is just ten cents a minute. You should know that from Jerusalem, it is merely a local call."

This simple joke reflects a greater truth: Jerusalem is the spiritual epicenter of the world—past, present, and future. It truly is a sliver of heaven on earth and is undeniably central to God's heart.

If I forget thee, O Jerusalem, let my right hand forget her cunning. (Ps. 137:5 KJV)

Can a mother forget her nursing child? Can she feel no love for the child she has borne? But even if that were possible, I would not forget you! See, I have written your name on the palms of my hands. (Isa. 49:15–16 NLT)

Prophetically, *Rosh Hashanah* is a call to regather and restore the children of Israel. When the ram's horn sounds, God will gather Israel from the four corners of the earth and bring the Jews back to the land, as the prophet Isaiah states: "It will also come about in that day, a great *shofar* will be blown. Those perishing in the land of Assyria and the exiles in the land of Egypt will come and worship ADONAI on the holy mountain in Jerusalem" (Isa. 27:13).

After about two thousand years, Isaiah's prophecy finally began to be fulfilled in the twentieth century. One of the most significant signs of the times is the establishment of Israel as a nation in 1948. Against all the odds, Israel became an independent nation fulfilling thousands of years of prophecy. God fulfilled His Word, and He sovereignly gathered His people from all four corners of the earth—South America, Russia, Ethiopia, the Middle East, Europe—ending thousands of years of exile. Today, there are more Jewish people in Israel than any other place in the world. Historically, nothing like this has happened since the return from the Babylonian exile.

On a separate but very significant note, Smith Wigglesworth, a British healing evangelist who was one of the pioneers of a groundbreaking Pentecostal revival that occurred over a century ago, prophesied that there would be a healing revival in the United States. The year President Harry Truman signed his support of Israel becoming a state in 1948 is the same year the prophesied revival broke out in America and lasted into the next decade. This revival reminds me of the passage from Genesis 12:3: "My desire is to bless those who bless you [Israel]."

As God resurrected the land of Israel, so too was her language restored. Hebrew was considered a dead language, meaning that prayer and study were its only uses. It was no longer spoken. However, today, it is the spoken language of the land brought back from the dead. In an article I read in a quarterly journal, the first president of the Republic of Ireland took a trip to Israel in 1958 on the tenth anniversary of Israel's nationhood. He commented, "In my eyes, your most extraordinary achievement is your success in reviving a language that had been dead for 2,000 years—Hebrew." The Irish president lamented that Ireland gained independence from England and could not regain its national language of Gaelic. However, in a decade, Israel restored what was lost for millennia. This restoration is undoubtedly a sign of God's prophetic plan unfolding. God has been in the process of physically regathering Israel in preparation for an extraordinary spiritual restoration and revival.

RETURNING TO LIFE

Rosh Hashanah is a sweet foretaste of the celebration of the messianic Kingdom to come. It is a reminder that we must prepare ourselves for the final call and blast. Jesus will descend upon the sound of the *shofar*, and there will be everlasting life. First Thessalonians 4:16 exhorts us:

> For the Lord himself will come down from heaven, with a loud command, with the voice of the archangel and with the trumpet call of God, and the dead in Christ will rise first. (NIV)

In Ezekiel 37, we see the valley of the dry bones. God asks His prophet Ezekiel a question: "Can these bones live?" And Ezekiel replies, "Sovereign LORD, you alone know" (v. 3 NIV). Then, God instructs Ezekiel to speak words of life to the bones, and the bones begin to join together. Muscle and tissue clothe them. Next, the breath of God comes in like the very *ruach* (breath) the Creator first blew into Adam and Eve as He formed them from the dust of the earth. The very breath of life causes these dry bones to be raised from the dead and to gather to build a great army.

It's important to understand that in this passage, God's restoration of Israel takes place in two stages. First, there is the physical regathering. The Lord brings the dispersed bones back together and reunites them. This regathering is the stage the children of Israel have been experiencing since 1948. The second phase is spiritual regeneration. The bones as we saw don't live until God's breath comes into them. This divine breath is symbolic of the spiritual revival and transformation that will occur among the Jewish people when they recognize Yeshua as the Messiah. The restoration of Israel will only fully happen when these two stages are complete.

What the Lord is going to do for Israel He can do for each of us on a spiritual level. As the *shofar* is blown on *Rosh Hashanah*, envision God breathing upon us. He wants to resurrect the parts of us that have died—the dead dreams, the failed plans, the hopes deferred. As Proverbs warns, "Hope deferred makes the heart sick, but a desire fulfilled is a tree of life" (13:12 ESV).

God wants to resurrect your dreams and destiny. In this time and season, He will breathe hope into the deepest chasm of your being, planting the seeds of the tree of life to take root and grow. He wants to restore you and regather you to Himself.

In Jewish thought, the *shofar* sounds because God wants us to be awakened and not fall asleep to this reality. Like Ezekiel's great army, God has mighty plans for your life, plans to prosper you, to give you a bright future and a renewed hope. Rest also in this reality: More than we desire God, He desires us. More than we pursue Him, He will chase after us. All we have to do is throw Him a sideways glance, and He will come running. Friends, the best is always yet ahead in God, as we go from glory to glory (2 Cor. 3:18).

God will regather not only the Jewish people at the sound of the *shofar* but also the church. As I shared earlier, there will be a final *shofar* blast that leads to God regathering all believers to Himself by resurrecting the living and dead at the Second Coming. Rabbi Paul wrote about this in 1 Thessalonians:

> For the Lord Himself shall come down from heaven with a commanding shout, with the voice of the arch-angel and with the blast of God's *shofar*, and the dead in Messiah shall rise first. Then we who are alive, who are left behind, will be caught up together with them in the clouds, to meet the Lord in the air—and so we shall always be with the Lord. Therefore encourage one another with these words. (4:16–18)

This raises the question, "Will you be ready when the *shofar* sounds?" May that day come speedily and soon!

HOW TO CELEBRATE
Rosh Hashanah

You will need:

- Dinner
- 2 candles and candlesticks
- Wine
- *Challah* bread
- Sliced apples
- Honey
- Body of water

Step 1: Start the celebration

Clear your schedule. *Rosh Hashanah* falls on a different day each year, usually in September. The two-day celebration begins at sundown the evening before the first full day.

Step 2: Have a family dinner

A family dinner on the first night begins the holiday. The meal may include *gefilte* fish, *matzo* ball soup, roast chicken or brisket, carrot *tzimmes*, and pomegranate. Greet everyone by proclaiming, "*L'Shanah Tovah!*" which in Hebrew means "For a good year!"

Step 3: Recite blessings

Light the candles and recite the ritual blessings over them. Recite the *kiddush,* or blessing, over the wine and the blessing over the *challah* bread. Pass the *challah* around for everyone to break off a piece and dip the bread and slices of apples in honey, symbolizing the hope that the new year will be sweet.

The circular shape of the *challah* bread represents the cycle of the year and of life.

Step 4: Go to a messianic synagogue

Go to the temple. Most synagogues feature an all-day program that includes songs, prayers, readings, sermons, and the story of the binding of Isaac from the *Torah.*

One of the holiday's *mitzvot,* or commandments, is to hear the ram's horn or shofar, which serves as a call to examine your behavior.

Step 5: Cast off your sins

After services, follow the rabbi to a flowing body of water for a ritual known as *Tashlich.* Some *Tashlich* ceremonies include tossing bits of bread into the water to symbolize letting go of and fully releasing your sins.

Step 6: Enjoy your year

Reflect on the past year and the year to come. Take time to remember those less fortunate, and include charitable giving in your *Rosh Hashanah* celebrations.

The Bible refers to Rosh Hashanah as *Yom Ha-Zikkaron*, day of remembrance, or *Yom Teruah*, day of shofar blowing.

The Jewish New Year, *Rosh Hashanah*, is followed by ten days of repentance and awe, culminating in *Yom Kippur*. Whereas *Rosh Hashanah* focuses on the repentance of the individual, *Yom Kippur* shares this focus and goes one giant step further: this holiday atones for the nation's sins. *Yom Kippur* is called the Day of Atonement.

CHAPTER FIVE

YOM KIPPUR

Adonai *spoke to Moses, saying: "However, the tenth day of this* *seventh month is* Yom Kippur, *a holy convocation to you, so* *you are to afflict yourselves. You are to bring an offering made* *my fire to* Adonai. *You are not to do any kind of work on that* *set day, for it is* Yom Kippur, *to make atonement for you before* Adonai *your God. For anyone who does not deny himself*

111

on that day must be cut off from people. Anyone who does

any kind of work on that day, that person I will destroy from

among his people. You should do no kind of work. It is a statute

forever throughout your generations in all your dwellings. It is

to be a Shabbat *of solemn rest for you, and you are to humble*

your souls. On the ninth day of the month in the evening—

from evening until evening—you are to keep your Shabbat."

Leviticus 23:26–32

The Jewish New Year, *Rosh Hashanah*, is followed by ten days of repentance and awe, culminating in *Yom Kippur*. Whereas *Rosh Hashanah* focuses on the repentance of the individual, *Yom Kippur* shares this focus and goes one giant step further: this holiday atones for the nation's sins. *Yom Kippur* is called the Day of Atonement.

The word *atonement* means "to make reparation for wrongdoing or injury." However, for reparation to take place, forgiveness must happen first. We can look upon forgiveness as the topsoil in which reparation can take root and flourish. A leading secular psychiatrist, Dr. Karl Menninger, stated that forgiveness is one of the critical needs of humanity. He went as far as to say that if he could convince the patients in psychiatric hospitals that their sins were forgiven, 75 percent could walk out the next day.[1] The power of forgiveness is unbelievable.

---

1 Dr. Elu Akpala Onnekikami, *The Divine Cure for a Broken Heart* (New York: iUniverse, 2006), 11.

Menninger's statement shocks us into realizing how powerful, even primal, this need is. Why? We were designed for connectedness, for relationship. Unforgiveness toward others, ourselves, and even God bears the bitter fruit of disconnection and separation. Separation is the root of most pain. It is a prison of isolation, whether physical, emotional, spiritual, or all of the above. Hell, both figuratively and literally, is separation. To the degree we feel separate, we suffer.

Being forgiven and forgiving others is the only way we can truly be free—free to love, free to connect and enjoy relationships with others, with ourselves, and with God. When we don't forgive, we might as well be physically bound to a dead weight that we drag around into everything we do and everywhere we go. Remember that movie *Weekend at Bernie's*, where two friends find the dead body of their boss and, for their own purposes, drag the body around pretending that he is alive? This dead weight physically burdens every move they make, which adds emotional and situational strain. Unforgiveness is like the dead body—it doesn't get any easier but becomes more burdensome as time goes by, wearying the bearer.

A compelling example of the tie that freedom has to forgiveness is found in the book *The Sunflower* by Simon Wiesenthal. During the Holocaust, Wiesenthal's work detail was assigned to clean up medical waste at a hospital for German soldiers. A nurse asked him if he was a Jew. When he answered yes, she led him to the bedside of a dying twenty-one-year-old Nazi. The Nazi wanted to die in peace, and he asked Wiesenthal, on behalf of the Jewish people, to forgive him and his horrible deeds. Simon could only offer the Nazi silence; then he left the room to the soldier's pleas for pardon. When Wiesenthal walked out of that room, I believe a part of him never recovered from the trauma of that experience. He was haunted for the rest of his life and wrote to many religious leaders asking them if he had done the right thing, as if he were looking for absolution. He even asked the readers at the end of *The Sunflower* whether they thought he made the right choice.

My point is not to condemn Mr. Wiesenthal by any means but to show how burdened he was by unforgiveness. He carried it around with him for the rest of his life. His response was very understandable, and really, forgiveness wasn't truly his to give. However, what might have happened in his heart and spirit if he had made this gesture for the higher good and did extend forgiveness to this soldier, even if it was mostly empty? What freedom might Wiesenthal have experienced having made this move of such a divine nature?

I'm sure Wiesenthal asked these questions of himself. However, the ultimate question is this: How wonderful would it have been if Wiesenthal had pointed this dying Nazi to the One who *could* offer complete forgiveness and freedom?

FORGIVENESS AND THE OLD TESTAMENT

For the life of the body is in its blood.
I have given you the blood on the altar to purify you,
making you right with the LORD.
It is the blood, given in exchange for a life,
that makes purification possible.
Leviticus 17:11 NLT

In the Old Testament on *Yom Kippur*, the Hebrews achieved forgiveness and atonement in the form of animal sacrifice. It was an exchange of life for life. This Day of Atonement was the single most hallowed day of the year when the *Kohein HaGadol*, the high priest, would enter into the Holy of Holies and say the sacred name of God. His focus and the focus of all Israel was on.

Repentance and Redemption . . .

The high priest fasted for twenty-five hours and afflicted his soul, which meant abstinence from certain pleasures, such as food, water, and marital relations. Since a little history never hurts, let's travel back to ancient Israel during *Yom Kippur* for a more in-depth understanding.

THE SCAPEGOAT

Of the various Day of Atonement sacrifices, the most central was that of the two he-goats. They were to be equal in height, weight, and cost. Next, lots were cast to determine which he-goat would be sacrificed as a sin offering upon the altar to the Lord and which one would be designated as the scapegoat "for Azazel."[2]

---

2 From *Harper's Bible Dictionary*, "A demonic figure to whom the sin-laden scapegoat was sent on the Day of Atonement (Lev. 16:8, 10, 26). The Hebrew word has been traditionally understood as a phrase meaning 'the goat that escapes,' giving us the word 'scapegoat.'"

The high priest laid his hands upon the head of the sacrificial goat in a gesture symbolizing the transference of sins from him, the nation's representative, to the animal, who would bear the burden. The priest would then fasten a scarlet, woolen cord to the horns of the goat and tie a second scarlet cord to the entrance of the *kodesh* section of the temple. Next, the high priest would lay both hands upon the scapegoat again, reciting the following confession of sin and prayer for forgiveness:

> O Lord, I have acted iniquitously, trespassed, sinned before Thee: I, my household, and the sons of Aaron Thy holy ones. O Lord, forgive the iniquities, transgressions, and sins that I, my household, and Aaron's children, Thy holy people, committed before Thee, as is written in the law of Moses, Thy servant, "For on this day He will forgive you, to cleanse you from all your sins before the Lord; ye shall be clean."[3]

The word *scapegoat* in our modern vernacular stems from ancient Israel. It means "a person who is blamed for the wrongdoings, mistakes, or faults of others." Accordingly, when the high priest would lay both hands on the scapegoat, he would transfer the iniquities of all Israel upon this hapless creature.

---

3 Isidore Singer, Ph.D., projector and managing editor, *The Jewish Encyclopedia: A Descriptive Record of the History, Literature, and Customs of the Jewish People From the Earliest Times to the Present Day*, vol. 2 (New York: Funk and Wagnalls Company, 1916), 367.

ALL INTEREST; NO PRINCIPAL

After all those present responded to this prayer, an individual was chosen, preferably a priest (*kohen*), to take the goat to the precipice in the wilderness, where the scapegoat would be thrown over a steep and jagged cliff, so that its body would be completely torn apart before it reached the bottom.

Once the sacrifice was complete, a *supernatural phenomenon* occurred. The red cords that were tied to the horns of the scapegoat and placed at the entrance of the Holy Place supernaturally turned from red to white to symbolize that although Israel's sins were as crimson, God has washed them as white as snow (Isa. 1:18). When this occurred, it publicly bore testimony that Israel had been forgiven.

Elaborating on the spiritual purpose of the scapegoat, Rabbi Moshe Alshich, a prominent sixteenth-century biblical commentator, taught that the scapegoat does not entirely wipe out Israel's sin. It only prevents the negative consequences of sin from being manifested against the people. What is true of the scapegoat is true of all the sacrifices offered on the Day of Atonement—they only provided a covering for Israel's sins but did not remove them altogether.

To put it in monetary terms, think of the holiday season when you spend too much money, receive the credit card bill, and gasp, "I can't believe that I spent so much!" You know that you cannot afford to pay off the credit card, so what do you do? You just pay the minimum, which only covers the interest and keeps the collection department from calling. But if you only pay the interest, you never wipe out the principal. The sacrifices in the Hebrew Bible parallel this: they merely covered the minimum, the interest, rather than the principal.

PAID IN FULL

In Leviticus 17:11 God states that life is in the blood. Without the shedding of blood—in Jewish thought—there would be no remission of sin. God sent the Messiah to pay the interest and principal in full.

The scapegoat represented the sins of the nation; *Yom Kippur* points to the ultimate redemption of the world, the fullness of redemption. A redemption is paid for, not by the blood of an animal, which still leaves a deficit, but by Yeshua's blood, marking the debt PAID IN FULL.

The sacrifice of the goat had supernaturally turned the crimson cord white, but this supernatural phenomenon STOPPED after the sacrifice of Jesus. According to the central text of rabbinic Judaism, the *Talmud*, forty years before the destruction of the temple in AD 70, the scarlet cord stopped turning from red to white. This would be around the time of Jesus' crucifixion and resurrection. This lack of color change is proof that the *Yom Kippur* sacrifices were no longer effective (Talmud, Tractate *Yoma* 39b). The he-goats offered by the high priest could not compare to Yeshua's ultimate offering.

What shall we say about such wonderful things as these? If God is for us, who can ever be against us? Since he did not spare even his own Son but gave him up for us all. (Rom. 8:31–32 NLT)

Greater love has no one than this: to lay down one's life for one's friends. (John 15:13 NIV)

The Promise of Reparation . . .

WE BROKE IT; HE FIXED IT

Man broke the world, in a sense, when he plucked that forbidden fruit from the tree. The eating of that fruit had a domino effect that resulted in a disconnection with God, others, self, and even creation, which is reflected in Paul's writings in Romans:

> The creation looks forward to the day when it will join God's children in glorious freedom from death and decay. For we know that all creation has been groaning as in the pains of childbirth right up to the present time. (Rom. 8:21–22 NLT)

We took something off the tree, so God put something back on the tree—His crucified body—to make restitution, to bring life, and to usher in blessing. What was broken by the first Adam was repaired by the second Adam, Yeshua-Jesus. This time, it was God's life for our life. God put His blood on the altar instead of an animal's blood or our blood as a FINAL sacrifice—"God set forth Yeshua as an atonement, through faith in His blood" (Rom. 3:25).

As God mended our broken relationship with Him, He called us to be fixers, restorers, repairers of the world. *Yom Kippur* focuses on this *reparation*. If we break a relationship with others, we have a responsibility to mend it. Whatever is in disrepair—relationships, ourselves, creation—we are called to repair and bring to a level of complete transformation and renewal. Remember, though, that for reparation to happen, forgiveness must occur first.

In Matthew 18:22, Jesus tells us to forgive those who have sinned against us: "Not up to seven times . . . but seventy times seven!" In the Sermon on the Mount in Matthew 5:23–24, Jesus instructs, "Therefore, if you are offering your gift at the altar and there remember that your brother or sister has something against you . . . First go and be reconciled to them; then come and offer your gift" (NIV).

In Judaism, if a person we need to forgive or need forgiveness from is dead, we go to their grave and perform a special ritual. There is a story in which a Holocaust survivor was planning to come to America. Before he left his homeland, he went to Hitler's grave. When asked why he did that, he replied, "I didn't want to take Hitler to America with me." He didn't want to drag the dead body of unforgiveness into his new life.

A few years ago, several people wronged me. I felt very hurt and betrayed. Right before *Yom Kippur*, God told me that I had to write a letter to them and ask for forgiveness if I had done anything wrong against them. I was not happy with that instruction. I told God, "I don't believe I did anything wrong, but they did." The Lord said to me, "Do you want to be right or righteous?" Then God said, "While you were still a sinner, I made the first move toward you." God wanted me to make the first move toward them.

There is another story that exemplifies the divine beauty of forgiveness, reflecting its transcendent nature. Richard Wurmbrand was a Romanian Jew who was converted to Christianity by a godly village carpenter in the late 1930s. Following his conversion, Wurmbrand became a pastor. Romania allied with Germany against the USSR in 1941, and Nazi forces filled the country. Richard and his wife, Sabina, purposed to evangelize the soldiers, even when the occupying forces killed Sabina's family.

One night, a Nazi came to their home; he had participated in the destruction of the village where Sabina's family lived. Richard treated him kindly; Sabina was sick in the other room. Richard challenged the soldier, "I propose to you a test. I promise that if I inform my wife about who you are and what you've done, she will not speak one word of unkindness to you. Even though you are guilty of this atrocity against her family, she will show you love in return. We've been forgiven by God and have experienced His grace and love. She will show you the same."

The Nazi was taken aback. Richard assured this soldier that his wife would recognize the pain and darkness of soul in the man's eyes and show him the sweetness of God. When he heard this, the Nazi broke down and sobbed uncontrollably, realizing his horrific deeds in the presence of this sublime goodness. Richard led him to the Lord right there, and then into where his wife was lying. Sabina was kind and loving to the soldier, even though she was made aware of his part in killing her loved ones. This forgiveness so transformed the soldier that he returned to his Nazi brothers and spent the rest of the war risking his life to rescue Jews instead of murdering them.

The bottom line is this: with God, forgiveness is not an elective but a requirement, not to stress us but to bless us. He wants us free rather than captive, transformed rather than imprisoned. In the book of Hebrews, Yeshua offered us complete forgiveness/atonement through His broken body "for the joy set before Him" (12:2). Relationship with us is the joy set before Him. Living from freedom allows us to experience this joy, which births relationship and oneness with God, with others, and with ourselves. Remember, Jesus said in John 15:2 that He wanted His joy to be in us so that our "joy may be complete" (NIV). We can't experience the fullness of His joy if we don't have His ability to forgive and be forgiven. When we genuinely experience forgiveness, both receiving and giving, we break free from the anchor that keeps us harbored in the dark waters of unforgiveness. In this forgiven/forgiving, transformed, free, joyous state, we experience the blessings of atonement, which can then be rewritten as *at-one-ment*.

GETTING IT RIGHT THE HUNDREDTH TIME

The world reveres the idea of getting things right the first time. Can you imagine if God had the same standards? Our Father knows our limitations. That is why He is the God of *many* chances. Throughout the Old and New Testaments, people blew it, and He blessed it.

For instance, Moses spent forty days and nights on Mount Sinai receiving the Ten Commandments from the finger of God. When he came down the mountain and found the Israelites worshiping a golden calf, he shattered the tablets in a fit of rage. God

could have huffed and puffed and blown their idol down and destroyed them all. Instead, He listened to Moses' pleas on behalf of his people and partnered with Moses to create a second set of Ten Commandments. This time, God dictated, and Moses carved the commandments into the stone tablets with his own hands.

In Jewish thought, because of this partnership between heaven and earth, the second set of tablets are believed to be more significant than the first. That is not to infer by any means that the first set was flawed. However, the hand of man, Moses, inscribing the words of God reflects the divine intention of the Father to co-labor with us, His children.

A little-known fact is that Moses came down from Mount Sinai with the second set of tablets on *Yom Kippur*. Nothing is random with God, friends. This intentional completion and delivery of the new tablets is a display of God repairing, *atoning* for, what's been broken. It is interesting to note that they housed the shattered tablets in the Ark with the intact ones. Why? Don't we throw away broken things since they are past their point of usefulness?

The answer is yes by the world's standards. However, God places the broken next to the whole to show the connection between them. Wholeness comes from brokenness. If we look at times in our lives where we've been broken, we can see the growth and transformation that resulted from those periods.

I went through a personal desert—no job, no income. Everything I planned didn't work out. It was my Joseph period. However, out of that time came the various ministries that I've established. I've spoken to recovered alcoholics that profess that recovery was challenging. However, they wouldn't pass up the opportunity for what they learned during the transition from brokenness to wholeness.

When we don't throw away our hard times but keep them next to our good times in the "Ark" of our memory, humility and wholeness result. Humility and wholeness allow us to stay sympathetic to those around us going through the same issues. They keep us compassionate. The co-existence of the two sets of tablets in the Ark reminds us of God's compassion, which turns brokenness into blessings.

Yeshua is the ultimate embodiment of the compassionate heart of God. Theirs was a divine co-laboring between Father and Son, between heaven and earth, culminating in the greatest act of compassion of all time—Yeshua's final atonement on our behalf.

WHY REMEMBER?

Why then should we celebrate *Yom Kippur* today when Messiah Yeshua is the ultimate atonement for sin? In Jewish tradition, between *Rosh Hashanah* and *Yom Kippur*, God determines whose names will be written in the Book of Life for another year. By celebrating *Yom Kippur*, we remember and give thanks that we have been inscribed not for one year but eternally in the Book of Life through the Messiah's death. Yeshua Himself said, "Do not rejoice that the spirits submit to you, but rejoice that your names are written in heaven" (Luke 10:20 NIV). By understanding and observing *Yom Kippur*, we remember and proclaim Messiah Yeshua to Israel and the nations. We declare that He is the one through whom final atonement, the forgiveness of sins, and eternal life are made available to all through faith in Him. Secondly, on *Yom Kippur*, we stand in the gap for Israel and the nations of the world that have not yet experienced the redemption and blessings that come through Yeshua's death. Like Abraham who interceded for Sodom (Gen. 18), like Daniel who identified with the corporate sins of Israel and pleaded for forgiveness (Dan. 9), and like our Great High Priest, Yeshua, who lives to make constant intercession for us, we have the responsibility to follow their examples and intercede on behalf of Israel and the nations.

Yom Kippur should also be important to all Jewish and Gentile followers of the Messiah because of its future prophetic fulfillment. On one level, the Messiah's death on the cross changed how we receive atonement. But there is also a promise in Scripture concerning the Jewish people's redemption, as the apostle Paul writes:

> For I do not want you, brothers and sisters, to be ignorant of this mystery—lest you be wise in your own eyes— that a partial hardening has come upon Israel until the fullness of the Gentiles has come in; and in this way all Israel will be saved, as it is written, "The Deliverer shall come out of Zion. He shall turn away ungodliness from

Jacob. And this is My covenant with them, when I take away their sins." Concerning the Good News, they are hostile for your sake; but concerning chosenness, they are loved on account of the fathers—for the gifts and the calling of God are irrevocable. (Rom. 11:25–29)

Atonement has been supplied, but it has not been fully applied to "all Israel" for her salvation. But at the end of days, Israel will come under its greatest persecution in her darkest hour. But, there is a marvelous ray of promise and hope according to the prophet Zechariah, who prophesies:

> "Then I will pour out on the house of David and the inhabitants of Jerusalem a spirit of grace and supplication, when they will look toward Me whom they pierced. They will mourn for him as one mourns for an only son and grieve bitterly for him, as one grieves for a firstborn." (Zech. 12:10)

And as result of their repentance and confession, the children of Israel and the land are cleansed and purified from their transgression and spiritual uncleanliness as described in the opening of the next chapter in the book of Zechariah:

> "In that day a spring will be opened to the house of David and to the inhabitants of Jerusalem to cleanse them from sin and impurity. It will happen in that day"—it is a declaration of *ADONAI-Tzva'ot* [LORD of Hosts]—"that

I will erase the names of the idols from the land and they will no longer be remembered." (Zech. 13:1–2)

Only when this occurs will *Yom Kippur* find its ultimate prophetic fulfillment, which is that "on this day atonement will be made for you, to cleanse you. From all your sins you will be clean before ADONAI" (Lev. 16:30). This prophetic fulfillment is a vital part of the final redemption that culminates in the establishment of the messianic Kingdom. The Kingdom is prophetically fulfilled in the Feast of Tabernacles (as we will see in the next chapter). By celebrating *Yom Kippur*, even as Yeshua and His disciples did, we demonstrate our faith, hope, and desire for Israel and the nations to experience the full and final redemption.

HOW TO CELEBRATE
Yom Kippur

1. **Prepare yourself the day before.** *Yom Kippur*, the Day of Atonement, is a full day of prayers and thought. The tradition of fasting for the twenty hours of the holiday underlines this spiritually meaningful day. This fast includes everything, even water. There are five prohibitions from which we abstain to fulfill the commandment to "afflict [our] souls" (Leviticus 16:29–30). Traditional Judaism interprets these verses to mean eating and drinking, but there is also no anointing oneself with perfumes or oils, no bathing for pleasure, and no wearing of leather shoes (making sure that there is no barrier between the feet and the ground to feel the pain of the pebbles, just like Moses was commanded to take off his shoes when he stood in the presence of the Lord. The high priest wore no shoes to identify with the people since the soles of the feet are the most sensitive part of the body. Shoes are also a barrier to connecting with the earth, which represents a connection to God and others). We also abstain from marital relations. The only exception to any of this fasting is if you are taking

medication. Otherwise, you are not allowed any of the items above. This abstinence is an attempt to focus your mind on spiritual things, like the angels in heaven. There is also a tradition for men and women to wear white. Religious Jews wear a white shroud known as a *kittel*, as white represents both purity and the angelic.

2. **Get yourself into the mindset of *Yom Kippur*.** The *Torah* has a very specific concept of repentance and atonement. It is both biblical and essential in Jewish tradition that you must atone for the sins you committed against your fellow man before you can even think about approaching God for the forgiveness of sins committed against Him. It is typical for Jews on the days approaching *Yom Kippur* to contact people whom they feel they have wronged during the year to seek atonement. As followers of Yeshua, we should all approach those we have hurt or who have wronged us to make amends. As a rabbi, Yeshua teaches in the Sermon on the Mount to get things right with your brother before making the sacrifice:

> "So if you are presenting a sacrifice at the altar in the Temple and you suddenly remember that someone has something against you, leave your sacrifice there at the altar. Go and be reconciled to that person. Then come and offer your sacrifice to God." (Matt. 5:23–24 NLT)

3. **Find out about services in your area.** *Yom Kippur* is one of the holiest and most significant holidays of the year and is best observed in community with other people of faith at a local messianic synagogue or congregation. The support will aid you throughout the day. An environment like a congregation or synagogue is also more conducive to focus and meditation. *Yom Kippur* begins at sundown on 10 Tishrei on the Hebrew calendar but is different every year on the Gregorian calendar. This holiday has the highest attendance of observance of the Jewish calendar year.

4. **Decide which services you want to attend.** The first service of the *Yom Kippur* holiday is called *Kol Nidrei* service, named after the main prayer said during the service. The *Kol Nidrei* is the most popular service and is traditionally performed at sundown. The next morning, there will be morning services. The *Musaf* service follows it. The afternoon service traditionally follows with readings from the book of Jonah.[4] The closing service—happening at sundown—is called *Neilah*. This service always ends with the blowing of the *shofar*.

---

4 The sages cite four reasons for the reading of the book of Jonah: (1) The book reminds us of God's infinite mercy. (2) The book corresponds to repentance, a profound theme of *Yom Kippur*. (3) The book serves as a reminder that the entire world and all of its natural forces are in God's hands. (4) The afternoon service is believed to be especially poignant for having prayers answered—we are reminded that we too can be saved, even as the day begins to wane. Excerpted from: https://www.myjewishlearning.com/article/jonah-yom-kippur/.

5. **Celebrate *Yom Kippur*.** Even though joyous celebration is usually not the tone of *Yom Kippur*, both choirs and the congregation sing beautiful songs. As mentioned before, the *Kol Nidrei* is the first opportunity for you to celebrate with your congregation. The *Kol Nidrei* prayer is often sung during the first part of this service with great embellishment and can be very moving. Your celebration of the holiday is the continuation and observance of your fast throughout the twenty-four-hour period. You can supplement this by attending the additional services that are available throughout the day on *Yom Kippur* proper. Finally, at the end of *Yom Kippur* at sundown, it is common to gather with friends and family to break the fast. It is traditional to celebrate the breaking of the fast with a hearty spread of food. The meal may include *challah*, bagels with cream cheese, and other Jewish delicacies like lox (smoked salmon).

6. **Understand the specific customs of the sect of Judaism whose synagogue you are attending.** If you are attending a more traditional *Yom Kippur* service, many,

if not all, men will be wearing a *kittel*—a white robe that covers the entire body. It is to be worn on the day of your wedding, during *Yom Kippur*, and when you are buried. Also, the traditional black *yarmulke* is white on *Yom Kippur*.

Note:

Leviticus 23 and Isaiah 58 teach us about afflicting our souls during *Yom Kippur* (Isaiah 58 is the *Torah* reading during *Yom Kippur*). During this season, we focus on charity and justice for the poor. It is an excellent idea on *Yom Kippur* to give to a justice-focused cause.

Sukkot celebrates God tabernacling among the children of Israel during their forty years in the wilderness as His presence led them as a cloud of smoke by day and as a pillar of fire by night.

CHAPTER SIX

Sukkot
THE FESTIVAL OF TABERNACLES

The LORD said to Moses, "Say to the Israelites: 'On the fifteenth day of the seventh month the LORD's Festival of Tabernacles begins, and it lasts for seven days. The first day is a sacred assembly; do no regular work. For seven days present food offerings to the LORD, and on the eighth day hold a sacred assembly and present

> *a food offering to the LORD. It is the closing special*
>
> *assembly; do no regular work.'"*
>
> Leviticus 23:33–36 NIV

We know that a Jewish holiday marked every milestone in the Messiah's life. He died on Passover. He arose on Firstfruits. Have you ever thought, *On which Jewish holiday was God Incarnate born?* It certainly wasn't Christmas.

I believe that the Messiah was born not on December 25 but during the Feast of Tabernacles, also known as *Sukkot*. This holiday is celebrated over eight days in the month of *Tishrei* on the Jewish calendar. It falls around late September or October on the Gregorian/Western Calendar. Did this blow your mind? Let me explain why I, like a growing number of people, believe this to be true.

Sukkot is one of three Jewish holidays that require a pilgrimage to Jerusalem. It would make sense that the Romans would take a census when all Jewish people were journeying to the Holy City. A census required everyone to return to the place of their birth to be registered. So *Sukkot* would be a perfect time to have people stop at their birthplaces on their way to Jerusalem. It would also make sense that with the crowds of people converging on the City of David, Bethlehem—which can be considered a suburb—would be filled with overflow. Most assuredly, there would be no room in the inn.

Sukkot celebrates God tabernacling among the children of Israel during their forty years in the wilderness as His presence led them as a cloud of smoke by day and as a pillar of fire by night. In light of this, there is a heightened theological significance of John 1:14: "And the Word became flesh and tabernacled among us." Yeshua-Jesus was born on *Sukkot*, for He is *Emmanuel*, God among us, the presence of the Lord dwelling among His people once again like He did in the desert.

The Promise of Rejoicing . . .

IT'S PARTY TIME!

Rejoicing is the fundamental word that summarizes *Sukkot*. In Hebrew, *Sukkot* means "the time of our rejoicing." Jewish tradition says that if you did not have the opportunity to go to Jerusalem during *Sukkot* in the days when the temple stood, you have never seen true rejoicing. It was not material pleasures but a pure spiritual joy that illuminated the people and the city for eight days and nights—a true celestial celebration. What was the reason for the season?

If you have yet to notice, the Jewish people remember. We remember to learn from, honor, and celebrate what God has done for us in the past. We also remember to anticipate and get excited about what God is going to do for us in the future. *Sukkot* is the party that recalls God's presence, protection, and provision when our ancestors exited Egypt and wandered the desert for forty years. What better reason to rejoice?

Don't forget: what God did in the past He will do again in the future. He is the unchanging, unwavering Abba (Papa God) and lover of our souls. Because of this awareness, the Jewish people live in an environment of expectation. Maybe that is why they are so successful. As a people and nation, they are small. However, their accomplishments per capita are off the charts. Why? They know they are blessed, and because of this, they are expectant of good.

HIS PRESENCE AND PROTECTION

It is impossible to separate God's presence from His protection. The manifest presence of God was the glory that led the Jews during the desert days, forming a canopy of clouds over them. The presence of God enclosed Israel on all six sides—top, bottom, north, south, east, and west. His presence formed a cocoon of protection from all the natural threats of the wilderness—sun, sandstorms, scorpions, and snakes. By night, He shielded them

against the cold and lit their way as a column of fire.

Sukkot, or *sukkah* (singular), that observant Jews construct during the holiday are temporary shelters. Each has a roof and at least three walls that are made of plywood or canvas. Jews give up the luxury of their homes to spend seven days and nights living in these "booths." These shelters represent the canopy of clouds of glory that sheltered God's people during their forty years in the wilderness. *Sukkot* is symbolic of His tangible presence. On the Mount of Transfiguration, Peter responds to seeing Yeshua, with Moses and Elijah, by offering, "If you wish, I will put up three shelters [sukkot]—one for you, one for Moses and one for Elijah" (Matt. 17:4 NIV). He offers this because, to the Jews, *sukkot* (tabernacles) were linked to the manifest presence of God and are connected to the coming of the Messiah. They also relate to the establishment of the messianic Kingdom through the promised son of David, as the prophet Amos writes:

"In that day I will raise up David's fallen *sukkah*.
I will restore its breaches,
raise up its ruins,
and rebuild it as in days of old." (Amos 9:11)

This verse is read on *Sukkot* and underscores the connection between tabernacles, the Messiah, and the Kingdom.

Jewish tradition teaches that each of the different gifts God gave Israel during their time in the wilderness came on account of a different Israelite leader. Jewish thought says that the clouds of glory came because of Aaron, who was the high priest. He was also the worship leader of the Jewish people. Worship is the key to intimacy that ushers in the presence of God. The glory filled the tabernacle when they worshiped. Worship is the fast pass into the presence.

The burning bush is how God manifested His presence to Moses. Tradition holds that because of Moses, the fiery column was another expression of God's presence. Throughout Scripture, fire and light connect with a visible manifestation of God, which is why all the Jewish holidays begin with lighting candles.

HIS PROVISION

The provision of water that sprang forth from the rock was connected to Miriam. She is also considered a leader of Israel. Miriam's whole life is associated with water. The first thing we read about Miriam is that she is by the water. Miriam is the one who follows Moses as he is put in the water. She follows him along the Nile to make sure that her little brother, the future deliverer of Israel, is going to be safe. Miriam is most remembered when she picks up the tambourine and leads the people in dancing (Ex. 15:20–21) after God parts the *Yom Suf*, the Sea of Reeds, for His people but covers Pharaoh's army with the waters.

As a side note, I love the fact that Israel's leaders included a woman. God was telling a culture that undervalued women to take note of their worth in His eyes. It goes to follow that the first people to recognize the resurrected Messiah were women—Mary Magdalene and Mary, the mother of James. These two women were the first evangelists as they ran to the upper room to proclaim the good news that *He is risen*!

This rock that burst forth a fountain did so in response to Israel's cry when they were thirsty, "Spring up, O well!" (Num. 21:17). Jewish tradition states that streams would flow from this rock and create an oasis of living waters. The water-drawing ceremony the priests performed in the temple commemorated this provision. Every day, the priests would go down and draw waters out of the pool of Siloam. They would come back up carrying water singing and dancing until they poured the water out as a libation offering on the altar in the temple. Describing this joyous ceremony the Sages write:

> He who has not seen the rejoicing at the place of the water-drawing has never seen rejoicing in his life. At the conclusion of the first festival day of Tabernacles they descended to the court of the women where they had made a great enactment. There were there golden candlesticks with four golden bowls on the top of each of them and four ladders to each, and four youths drawn from the priestly stock in whose hands were held jars of oil ... there was not a courtyard in Jerusalem that was not illumined by the light of the place of the water-drawing. Men of piety and good deeds used to dance before them with lighted torches in their hands, and sing songs and praises. And Levites without number with harps, lyres, cymbals and trumpets and other musical instruments were there upon the fifteen steps leading down from the court of the Israelites to the court of the women, corresponding to the fifteen songs of ascents in the psalms. (Babylonian Talmud, Tractate *Sukkah* 51a and 51b)

On the seventh day, they marched around the altar seven times. They poured out the collected water as an offering, asking God to pour out the latter rains, symbolizing Israel's utter dependence on God for the right amount of rain for any food to be able to grow. It was not like Egypt, where the Nile watered the ground and made it fertile. They were dependent upon God for the early and latter rains.

It was also a reminder of the water God provided in the wilderness and a prayer that God would pour out redemption and His spirit upon all flesh as the prophets foretold (Isa. 12:2–3). Let's look at 1 Corinthians to see whom Paul claims the rock that gave the water in the wilderness to be:

> For I do not want you to be ignorant of the fact, brothers and sisters, that our ancestors were all under the cloud and that they all passed through the sea. They were all baptized into Moses in the cloud and in the sea. They all ate the same spiritual food and drank the same spiritual drink; for they drank from the spiritual rock that accompanied them, and that rock was **Christ** [Messiah]. (10:1–4 NIV)

Now, let's consider the John 7:37–39 passage below. See how Jesus refers to Himself during the last day of *Sukkot*.

> On the last and greatest day of the festival [Feast of Tabernacles], Jesus stood and said in a loud voice, "Let anyone who is thirsty come to me and drink. Whoever believes in me, as Scripture has said, rivers of living water will flow from within them." (NIV)

Yeshua is declaring He is the source of that water that they drank from in the wilderness and the only one who can provide them with the water they longed for! He is the rock, the fount, the source of provision for all who are in need.

THE MIRACLE OF THE *MANNA*

The Bible says that neither the Israelites' clothes nor their shoes wore out for forty years (Deut. 8:4). Can you imagine? The harsh conditions would have ruined those items in forty days had it not been for God's covering. He also turned a stone into a spring, as we've just discussed. Additionally, Abba/Father gave them the provision of bread from heaven. God meant for the *manna* in the wilderness to not only feed their bellies but also test their faith. See, there was only enough *manna* for each day. Every morning, they had to go out and collect it. If they tried to accumulate *manna* for multiple days, it would spoil. Only on *Shabbat* were they able to collect for two days without spoilage to observe the Sabbath. Part of the lesson to Israel was that they had to trust Him every day for their provision. In the Lord's Prayer, Yeshua asks, "Give us **today** our daily bread" (Matt. 6:11 NIV). Not this week, month, or year. Today. We have to trust him **daily**. That was the lesson of the *manna*.

I believe there is also another less obvious lesson of the *manna*: We cannot live off yesterday's bread. We cannot live off yesterday's accomplishments. We cannot live off yesteryear's achievements. It does not matter if they are spiritual or temporal. If we try and live off the past, it is like rotten, putrid *manna*. We remember the past; we thank God for the past. However, we have to trust Him for the daily provision of the here and NOW. He is steadfast. The Lord never ceases; His mercies never end; great is His faithfulness, for they are new every morning. His blessings are new every day. We cannot just be looking to the past—what we have done and had or where we have been. We have to be living in the present and looking to the future expectantly. We have to look for what God wants to do *today*. What if every morning we asked, "What is Your *manna* miracle today for me, Lord?" Wouldn't that delight His heart? Wouldn't that show the faith that the Bible tells us is the only way to please Him? We also must anticipate His goodness in our future based on His past performance. There is no way around it. Jeremiah 29:11 says, "For I know the plans I have in mind for you . . . plans for *shalom* and not calamity—to give you a future and a hope." Like He did with the children of Israel in the wilderness, God is testing the quality of our faith and dependence upon Him by how we live today and trust Him for our future.

PHYSICAL AND SPIRITUAL NOURISHMENT

In the Pentecost chapter, we learned how the *Torah* was connected with water according to Jewish thought. *Torah* and bread are also connected—water and bread feed the body as the *Torah* nourishes the soul. *Torah* and bread are also linked to Moses. He led the people out of Egypt, where *manna* showered from heaven to feed them. He gave them the *Torah* on Sinai to provide for them spiritually.

As the Messiah linked Himself to living water on the last day of *Sukkot* in John 7, so did He align Himself with bread in John 6:

Yeshua said to them, "I am the **bread of life**. Whoever comes to Me will never be hungry, and whoever believes in Me will never be thirsty." (v. 35)

Isn't it fitting that King David and Messiah Jesus were born in Bethlehem, which translates in Hebrew as "House of Bread"? One of Jesus' most remembered miracles is the multiplication of bread. He took five loaves and fed five thousand people. Just like Moses gave *manna* to Israel, Yeshua gave bread in the wilderness to the crowds that followed Him. He is the greater Moses, and this is a foretaste of the bread of the world to come that God is going to provide for us in the messianic times.

REMEMBERING AN ATTITUDE OF GRATITUDE

As we speak of provision and how God satisfies us physically and spiritually, it is interesting to note the two blessings that the Bible **requires**. Most people love the scene from *Fiddler on the Roof* as the townspeople acknowledge that in Judaism there is a blessing for everything and someone asks the rabbi, "Is there a proper blessing for the czar?" After thinking a bit, the rabbi retorts, "May God bless and keep the czar . . . far away from us." There is a blessing for everything—when we wake up, when we lie down, when we wear our new garment when we travel, and even when we go to the bathroom. There is a blessing for everything. The primary purpose is to perceive God in all things and thankfully acknowledge Him in the supernatural and the mundane—that everything we have is a blessing from God. Technically in the Scriptures, however, there are only two things that require a blessing. One of them is in Deuteronomy, which is the book that ends the *Torah* reading cycle during *Sukkot*.

> When you have eaten your fill, be sure to praise the LORD your God for the good land he has given you. (Deut. 8:10 NLT)

When we're fat and happy, we need to remember and bless Him from whom all good things flow: "Not by [your] might, nor by [your] power, but by My *RUACH* [Spirit]!" (Zech. 4:6). God knows the heart of man. When everything is going well, and people have all they possibly could desire, God becomes concerned for our well-being. Poverty is bad; wealth is dangerous. That is why Yeshua said, "It is easier for a camel to go through the eye of a needle, than for a rich man to enter into the kingdom of God" (Mark 10:25). When we are in abundance, we have to remember God and pray to Him with hearts as earnest and hungry as if we were in crisis. God wants us to prosper. He doesn't want to be forgotten amid the prosperity because He is eternal, where all else is temporal. Jesus, in Matthew 6:20, tells us, "Store up for yourselves treasures in heaven, where neither moth nor rust destroys and where thieves do not break in or steal."

The other required blessing is to bless God before reading His Word. As we go into the new *Torah* cycle, which comes at the end of *Sukkot*, the blessing says, "When I proclaim the name of the Lord, ascribe greatness to our God." Sages teach that we are responsible to bless God before we study the *Torah*. How many of you say a blessing before you study the Word of

God? Doesn't it make sense to be in prayer before going into His Word? How much can more revelation be gained if we are already in a prayerful state?

> Ezra opened the book in the sight of all the people for he was standing above all the people; and when he opened it, all the people stood up. Then Ezra blessed the LORD the great God. And all the people answered, "Amen, Amen!" while lifting up their hands; then they bowed low and worshiped the LORD with their faces to the ground. (Neh. 8:5–6 NASB)

Again, bread and *Torah* are associated in that they are the two required blessings in the Bible.

SIMCHAT TORAH!

Simchat Torah means "Rejoicing in the *Torah*." This holiday, celebrated as part of *Sukkot*, marks the completion of the weekly *Torah* readings. Each week in the synagogue, we read a few chapters from the *Torah* in community, starting with Genesis 1 and working our way throughout the year to Deuteronomy 34. I believe there is a great blessing for Christians to follow the weekly *Torah* portions as well. Yeshua-Jesus read the weekly *Torah* portion, and Paul, as well as all the apostles, went into a synagogue for the weekly *Torah* readings. They can be considered God's original Bible reading program.

On *Simchat Torah*, we read the last *Torah* portion and then continue immediately to the reading of the first chapter of

Genesis. This perpetual cycle reminds us that the *Torah* is a circle and never ends. This completion of the readings is a time of grand celebration. There are high-spirited singing and dancing processions around the synagogue, carrying the *Torah* scrolls, with as many people as possible given the honor of an *aliyah* (reciting a blessing over the *Torah* reading), including children. Also, as many people as possible are given the privilege of carrying a *Torah* scroll in these processions. Since the scrolls are heavy, children follow the procession around the synagogue, sometimes carrying small toy *Torahs* (stuffed plush toys or paper scrolls). This party celebrates the eternal Word of God, which contains the unwavering promises of God that underscore His constant presence and an endless supply of provision and protection.

THE SAME YESTERDAY, TODAY, AND FOREVER

Hebrews 13:8 is one of the underlying themes of this book. As mentioned at the beginning of this book, the events of the past that the Jewish holidays celebrate and commemorate are a mirror of future events. That can only be said if God is faithful and His love for us steadfast. We know that to be true. We also know that God's presence, protection, and provision are still as vibrant today as in biblical times. Look more recently to Israel's status as a nation and the provision and protection that have been their continuous heritage. The fact that we can call Israel a nation is a miracle in itself. Without going into a history lesson, international sympathy for the Jews following World War II was undeniable; the UN voted to partition Palestine in

1947. On May 14, 1948, the Jewish National Council proclaimed the State of Israel, and US recognition came within hours by President Harry Truman. The next day, outraged Arab forces from Egypt, Jordan, Syria, Lebanon, and Iraq invaded the new nation. By the ceasefire on January 7, 1949, Israel had increased its original territory by 50 percent.

Less than two decades later, these same disgruntled, neighboring forces, with the addition of Lebanon, poised for war against Israel again. According to all the military analysts, it was a lopsided match: the Israeli Defense Forces totaled 275,000 troops; the combined Iraqi, Syrian, Jordanian and Egyptian armies totaled 456,000 soldiers. The combined Arab forces boasted more than double the number of tanks and close to four times the amount of combat aircraft. With close to two and a half million Jews living in Israel, the tiny country had the highest concentration of Jews since pre-Holocaust Eastern Europe. Given the Goliath-sized odds stacked against them, the nation was earmarking national parks to become gravesites for the many who would perish during the war.

However, six short days later, the war ended, earning the title of the Six-Day War. In less than a week, the territory under Israeli control had tripled in size. Jews were able to settle in sites where their ancestors hadn't lived for thousands of years. The Jewish nation was miraculously victorious in the face of what should have been impossible. Military strategists never study wars concerning Israel because they don't study the miraculous, which warrants Israel's first prime minister David Ben-Gurion's statement, "In Israel, in order to be a realist, you must believe in miracles."[1] *Sukkot* is another holiday that celebrates the God of the impossible.

THE *SUKKOT* OF THE FUTURE

*Then all the survivors from all the nations that attacked
Jerusalem will go up from year to year to worship the
King, ADONAI-Tzva'ot [the LORD Almighty], and to
celebrate* Sukkot *[the Festival of Tabernacles].*
Zechariah 14:16

Sukkot is the only Jewish holiday, other than *Shabbat*, that is prophesied as the one that will be celebrated by all the nations in the messianic Kingdom to come. In fact, in the Lord's Prayer, when Jesus says, "Thy kingdom come," I believe He is referring to Zechariah 14:16, which paints the picture of the Kingdom of Yeshua-Jesus. It refers to the surviving Jews and Gentiles gathering in the City of David, the Holy City, to celebrate *Sukkot and the birth of Messiah Yeshua, which likely happened on this holy day.* I think Scripture makes it clear how important it is to unify with one another for the feasts. I also believe that the celebrations continue in the heavens. Remember, Yeshua-Jesus finished His prayer with this line: "on earth as it is in heaven." The celebration of *Sukkot* expresses our expectation and desire for the Messiah and His Kingdom to come! Since Jews and Gentiles will celebrate *Sukkot* in the Kingdom, it only makes sense to celebrate it now as we await that day!

---

1 Donna Rosenthal, *The Israelis: Ordinary People in an Extraordinary Land* (New York: Free Press, a division of Simon & Schuster, Inc., 2003), 97.

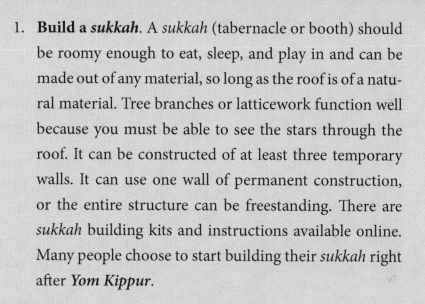

HOW TO CELEBRATE
Sukkot

1. **Build a *sukkah*.** A *sukkah* (tabernacle or booth) should be roomy enough to eat, sleep, and play in and can be made out of any material, so long as the roof is of a natural material. Tree branches or latticework function well because you must be able to see the stars through the roof. It can be constructed of at least three temporary walls. It can use one wall of permanent construction, or the entire structure can be freestanding. There are *sukkah* building kits and instructions available online. Many people choose to start building their *sukkah* right after ***Yom Kippur***.

2. **Decorate your *sukkah*.** Traditional decorations consist of harvest vegetables (corn, pumpkins, squash) hung from the ceiling and beams or placed in corners. Other decorations can include paper chains, pipe-cleaner constructions, pictures, wax paper stained glass, anything else that you or your children feel like creating. Children delight in being involved in the decoration of the *sukkah*.

3. **Shake the *lulav* and *etrog*.** A *lulav* is a single palm leaf, two willow branches, and three myrtle branches held together by woven leaves. An *etrog* is a lemon-like fruit grown in Israel. Hold the *lulav* in your right hand and the *etrog* in your left, say the blessing below over them, and then shake them in the six directions: north, south, east, west, up, and down, symbolizing God's presence everywhere.

Blessings for *Lulav* and *Etrog*:

Barukh atah ADONAI, Eloheinu, melekh ha-olam kidishanu b'mitz'votav v'tzivanu
Blessed are you, Lord, our God, sovereign of the universe who has sanctified us with His commandments and commanded us,

al n'tilat lulav (Amein).
to take up the *lulav* (Amen).

Shaking the *lulav* and *etrog* is a biblical commandment (known as a *mitzvah*) derived from Leviticus 23:40: "On the first day you are to take choice fruit of trees, branches of palm trees, boughs of leafy trees, and willows of the brook, and rejoice before ADONAI your God for seven days."

There is incredible spiritual symbolism and meaning behind the shaking of the *lulav* and *etrog*. On the most basic level, *Sukkot* is a fall harvest holiday. The waving of these four species of trees demonstrates and arouses thanksgiving and praise to the Lord for His gracious provision. Each element of the four species represent a different part of the body:

- The citron (*etrog*) represents the heart (i.e., mind and emotions).
- The palm branches (*lulav*) refer to the spine (i.e., the place where our actions come from as well as uprightness).
- The myrtle (*hadas*) is symbolic of the eyes and the desire to see only the good and to look upon the Lord.
- The willow has leaves that resemble the lips, which represent speech and prayer.

By bringing all four elements together we are symbolically demonstrating our desire and commitment to unite all the core aspects of our being to serve God with all our heart/mind, actions, eyes, and lips.

4. **Eat, drink, and be merry in your *sukkah*.** It is a *mitzvah* to eat in your *sukkah*, to play there, to sleep within its walls. Some people eat every meal in it and some sleep there for seven nights. This is more feasible in temperate climates when it is still warm at this time of year. *Sukkot* (the plural of *sukkah*) also make great houses for backyard children's games. The following prayer is said before eating a meal in the *sukkah*:

Barukh atah ADONAI, *Eloheinu, melekh ha-olam*
Blessed are you, LORD, our God, sovereign of the universe

asher kidishanu b'mitz'votav v'tzivanu
who has sanctified us with His commandments and commanded us

leisheiv basukah (Amein).
to dwell in the *sukkah* (Amen).

5. **Eat traditional *Sukkot* food.** As well as *holishkes*, which are stuffed cabbage leaves, the traditional food includes many types of stuffed vegetables.

6. **Leave your *sukkah* up until *Simchat Torah*, eight days.** You should not take it down until after *Simchat Torah* is over.

7. **Take your *sukkah* down and keep the materials for next year.** Store the materials in a safe place out of the way for next year's celebrations.

There are two aspects of the miracle of *Chanukah*: fighting and lighting. First, it reminds us of the miracle of impossibility—the underdog Maccabees were out-armed and extremely out-trained. Yet, they were the victors over the world power of the day. Secondly, the oil that was expected to burn for one day set the *menorah* aflame for eight days.

CHAPTER SEVEN

Chanukah
AND THE SEASON OF MIRACLES

It was now winter, and Jesus was in Jerusalem
*at the time of **Hanukkah**, the Festival of Dedication.*

John 10:22 NLT

The story of *Chanukah* reads like a fairy tale. A wicked Seleucid king by the name of Antiochus Epiphanes wanted to reunite the broken empire of Alexander the Great. To accomplish this task, he had to culturally unify the people around the common Hellenistic-Greco customs. He esteemed this culture to be the most civil and educated in the world. He also deemed Judaism to be a threat to this goal of unification. So, he outlawed the practice of Judaism.

To make matters worse, the king arrogantly stormed the temple, violating its most sacred space—the Holy of Holies. In a display of utter blasphemy, he publicly offered a pig sacrifice upon the altar. Not only was this not kosher, but it was a foreshadowing of the abomination of desolation that will occur in the end times (Dan. 9:27; Matt. 24:15–16).

Thumbing his pointy nose at the Jews in another confrontative move, Antiochus erected an idol to Zeus in the temple. Then, he ordered his emissaries to invade individual towns throughout the land of Israel. He commanded these henchmen to gather the leaders of the community and force them to offer sacrilegious sacrifices to the Greek gods.

In one town called *Modi'in*, a priest by the name of Mattathias, or *Matisyahu* in Hebrew, was asked to perform this profanity against his own will. He refused to commit this idolatrous act. However, another Jew stepped forward to make the offering.

Watching from the sidelines, Mattathias became so infuriated by what he saw that he grabbed a knife and violently killed this Jew who was willing to commit idolatry as well as the official who was supervising the blasphemy. This incident was the trigger for what history later recorded as the Maccabean Revolt. Mattathias's rallying cry was "Every one of you who is zealous for the law [*Torah*] and strives to maintain [has faith in] the covenant, follow me" (1 Maccabees 2:27).[1]

After Mattathias died a year later, his son Judah Maccabee gathered a ragtag bunch of Jewish renegades, now known as the Maccabees, and launched military guerilla warfare against the most powerful army of their day, the Greeks. After three and a half years, they won the war against impossible odds, proving Zechariah 4:6: "Not by might, nor by power, but by My *Ruach* [Spirit]!" As a sidenote, they fought against their foe the same amount of years that Jesus' earthly ministry lasted.

Riding high on victory and faith, these haphazard warriors went back to Jerusalem to recapture the temple. They found it decimated. Furthermore, the seven-branched candelabra called a *menorah* that was supposed to burn perpetually, symbolizing God's eternal presence and promise to the Jewish people, was extinguished. Determined to set this symbol ablaze again, they searched the trampled temple and found a *cruz*, or flask of oil. This oil was not ordinary but kosher oil of the purest kind.

There was one problem. This amount of oil would burn for only a day.

---

1 Naomi Pasachoff and Robert J. Littman, *A Concise History of the Jewish People* (Lanham, MD: Rowman & Littlefield Publishers, Inc., 1995), 52.

SUPERNATURAL PROVISION

This limited supply didn't deter the Maccabees. In a leap of faith, they lit the *menorah*. They rededicated the temple to God, which is why *Chanukah* is known as the Feast of Dedication. God blessed their act of faith and supernaturally stretched the one-day supply of oil to burn for eight days. This supernatural lighting is the great miracle that is commemorated each year during the *Chanukah* holiday, known by yet another name—the Festival of Lights.

THE MIRACLE OF *CHANUKAH*:
FAITH AND TRUST

There are two aspects of the miracle of *Chanukah*: fighting and lighting. First, it reminds us of the miracle of impossibility—the outnumbered, underdog Maccabees. They were out-armed and extremely out-trained. Yet, they were the victors over the world power of the day. Secondly, the oil that was expected to burn for one day set the *menorah* aflame for eight days.

You might ask, "Why would they even light it? Didn't it seem useless with such an insufficient supply?" The reasonable answer is yes. However, the Maccabees weren't thinking with their heads. They were thinking with their hearts of faith (*emunah*) and their trust in God (*bitachon*). If they had listened to their *reason*, they would never have lit the *menorah*. I can hear the enemy now: "Are you guys crazy? You Maccabees have been walloped in the head one too many times!"

Our heads are Satan's favorite playground and our worst battleground. You have heard the saying "You are what you eat." I'm going to add to that: you are what you believe. Bill Johnson states, "I can't afford to have a thought in my head about me that He doesn't have in His head about me."[2] Amen. The enemy seeks to enslave us into wrong thinking about God, ourselves, and the world around us. His goal is to make us believe lies. When we believe the lies, we empower the liar. Fear is an agreement with the liar and faith in the devil.

True faith is mental agreement with God. That is why Paul writes in Romans 12:2, "Do not be conformed to this world but be transformed by the renewing of your mind." God's commandment told the Maccabees to keep the *menorah* ablaze because the fire was never to go out of it. The *menorah* symbolized the presence and the promises of God to His people. Did those ever stop? No! So, they stepped out in faith and trust and lit the *menorah*, not knowing what would happen. One day of supply stretched into eight days of light as God delivered, delighted at how His people believed in and trusted Him.

TRUST IS FAITH WITH FEET

Faith is about belief. Trust goes one step further and puts feet on faith, moving us into action. It is not enough to know that God can slay giants; we must trust God enough to go out and slay them ourselves. That is the difference between faith and trust.

---

2 Bill Johnson, *God Is Good: He's Better Than You Think* (Shippensburg, PA: Destiny Image Publishers, Inc., 2018), eBook edition.

A well-respected rabbi distinguishes the difference between the two. He parallels faith and trust to two separate concepts, like two sides of the same coin.

They are inseparable. However, you can have faith *without* trust, but it is impossible to have trust without faith. Faith is the foundation upon which trust takes a stand.

> Blessed be the one who trusts in the LORD. The LORD shall be his confidence [*bitachon*]. He is like a tree planted by the water that sends out its roots by the stream. (Jer. 17:7–8, translation mine)

KRISTALLNACHT: NIGHT OF BROKEN GLASS

One of the most powerful and compelling stories of trust comes from Nazi Germany in 1938.

November 9 would become known as the "Night of Broken Glass," or *Kristallnacht*. This night earned this dubious distinction when Nazi thugs took to the streets all over Germany, destroying thousands of Jewish synagogues, cemeteries, and businesses. Many Jews were in denial. They could not believe that the country, which had allowed them decades of peace and prosperity, would make the persecution and murder of their Jewish citizens an official German policy.

However, Judah Geier was paying attention.

Kristallnacht compelled him to decide to leave his homeland with his family on Christmas Eve, 1938. He picked this Christian holiday hoping for a little relaxed security and some goodwill from German officials. It was also the eighth day of *Chanukah*, the culmination of the Jewish holiday. Judah was a cantor and devoted follower of the *Torah*. Never had his family not celebrated God's faithfulness and provision by lighting the *Chanukah* candles. This time, he and his family were traveling incognito, slinking out of town instead of lighting the *Chanukah* candles in defiance of the Nazis. Remorse consumed his thoughts as the train chugged out of the station toward incalculable dangers for Judah, his wife, Regina, and their two children, Arnold and Ruth.

Too soon for Judah, the train mercilessly approached the Dutch-German border. The Gestapo and the German police waited to inspect passports and travel papers. Judah nervously fingered the nine *Chanukah* candles in his pocket. While looking calm on the outside, the Geier family was feverishly aware that the wrong word or even a nervous glance could spell doom in just minutes. The train rattled and coughed to a stop. German officials on the ground huddled together, comparing passenger lists and checking assignments, while Judah and his family waited. The Geiers sat for a ten-minute eternity, nearly paralyzed with fear, before the Nazis entered the train.

Suddenly, they were all plunged into total darkness. The entire station, and every part of the train, inexplicably lost power. Without thinking, Judah pulled the candles out of his pocket and lined them up in the train's window. Traditionally, the candles are lit in a public place, such as a window, to bear witness to the miracle and bolster faith. So, he lit them one by one, setting apart the *shamash*, the ninth candle that lights the other eight, as is custom. The boots of the Gestapo thundered toward their train car. The frightened eyes of his family watched

Judah as he resigned himself to what may come and whispered the *Chanukah* blessing, "Blessed are you, our God, the Creator of time and space, who performed miracles for our ancestors in the days of long ago and in this time."

The door burst open with a bang, and the German officials flooded into the car. Judah readied himself. But he was not arrested. He was praised! The light of his candles would allow the Nazis, always the epitome of German efficiency, to proceed on schedule with checking papers. The chief of border police took only a cursory look at the Geier's papers before effusively thanking them for their resourcefulness and help.

The Germans, who considered Jews lower than dogs, had no reason to know it was *Chanukah* or recognize the candles as the lights of the Jewish festival. The Geiers were safe.

They sat in stunned awe at the God who had delivered them. With new and deeper meaning, their hearts focused on the candles for the next half hour. At the same time, German officials saw only utility lights to help them complete their tasks. As if on cue, just as the candles began to sputter out, the station lights flickered back on. "Judah, still in awe at what he had just witnessed, put his arm around his twelve-year-old son. With tears in his eyes, he drew him close. 'Remember this moment,' he declared softly. 'As in the days of the Maccabees, a great miracle happened here.'"[3] The train pulled out toward Amsterdam and freedom. Like the Maccabees, the Geier family now had a *Chanukah* miracle of their own.

---

3 Yitta Halberstam and Judith Leventhal, "A Holocaust Chanukah Miracle," The Jewish Woman.Org. As told by Arnold Geier (Judah's son) to Pesi Dinnerstein.

SPINNING OUT OF CONTROL, OR CENTERED ON GOD

One of *Chanukah*'s primary messages is for us to examine our hearts and ask: *In what are we putting our trust? Are we trusting in our abilities or God?* We must be people who are utterly dependent and **centered** on God alone.

Another symbol of this holiday, besides the *menorah*, is the *dreidel*: a four-sided top on which is inscribed "A great miracle happened there," referring to the Maccabean miracle. Many believe the *dreidel* was chosen as an icon of this holiday when the Greeks ruled over the Jewish people. Through the Seleucid empire, under the evil and wicked King Antiochus, the Jewish people were forbidden to study the *Torah* and to obey many of the *mitzvot*, the main commandments written in the *Torah*. When the children or people were studying, they would keep a *dreidel* nearby so that if the soldiers were to barge in, they would pretend that they were gathered not to learn but to gamble, which was popular among the Greeks in those days. After we light the *Chanukah* candles, we play this *dreidel* game and sing the children's rhyme:

I have a little *dreidel*. I made it out of clay.
When it's dry and ready, then *dreidel* I shall play.
Oh *dreidel, dreidel, dreidel,* I made it out of clay.
Oh *dreidel, dreidel, dreidel,* then *dreidel* I shall play.

It has a lovely body, with legs so short and thin.
When it gets all tired, it drops and then I win![4]

As with most everything in Judaism, there are more levels of meaning than meet the eye, even with the *dreidel*. Are you game for a mini Hebrew lesson? There are four Hebrew letters on each side of the cube: *Gimel*, *Nun*, *Shin*, and *Heh*. Every letter in Hebrew also corresponds to a number. If you add up the numerical value of each of these letters, they equal 358. Why is this significant? If you add up the letters in the word *Mashiach*, or Messiah, it also equals 358. The numerical value for the phrase "God reigns; God has reigned; God will reign [ADONAI *melech* ADONAI *malach* ADONAI *yimloch l'olam va'ed*]" totals 358 as well. The *dreidel* is not just a top but a symbol of our lives, spinning and circling whatever we choose to place at the center, which should be the Messiah.

GOING DEEP WITH THE *DREIDEL*

The Hebrew letters on the four sides of the *dreidel* also relate to the four basic dimensions of self. The letter *Gimel* refers to *guf*, which is the Hebrew word for the body. It refers to the material part of man. The letter *Nun* refers to *nefesh*, the spirit and the soul. It is that aspect of us that allows the body to feel, to develop, and to grow—even as Yeshua did "in wisdom and stature" (Luke 2:52). Next, *Shin* stands for mind and consciousness,

---

4 *Messianic Music Arrangements: Songs for Worship and Praise* (Yahshua Ben Yahweh Music, 2012), 109. For more information visit: https://jewishamericansongster.com/my-fathers-songs/.

an aspect of wisdom and common sense. Finally, there is *Heh*, which in Hebrew stands for "all," representing the transcendent part of the individual, which helps unite the other three.

Diving deeper still, there are four exiles of the Jewish people that, in Jewish thought, spiritually attacked the four different parts of the self. The Babylonians destroyed the first temple and exiled the Jewish people from Jerusalem. The purpose of the Babylonian exile was to extinguish the *Nun*, the *nefesh* of God's people. The Babylonians sought to annihilate the spiritual center of His people—the temple in Jerusalem.

After the Babylonian Empire, the Persian Empire reigned in power. This kingdom sought to destroy the *Gimel*, or *guf*. Who arose out of that kingdom? Haman! He tried to destroy the Jewish people physically by committing genocide.

After the Persian exile, the Greeks ransacked the Jewish people, intending to desecrate the *Shin*—the mind and consciousness. The Greek exile was a cultural attack on the intellect of God's people. They sought to indoctrinate God's people into a Hellenistic way of understanding the world. They forbade the Jews to study the *Torah* and to keep the *mitzvot*, the commandments. In Jewish thought, the mind and the heart are connected. The Greeks wanted to change the way the Jews fundamentally saw the world, their culture, and their traditions and how they understood God.

The Roman Empire sought to attack all three, thus the *Heh*. They destroyed the second temple, ushering in an attack on the body, mind, and spirit of God's people. Every aspect was under siege.

There is an inherent link between physical exile and spiritual exile. The chaos and disorder, the uprooting and upheaval of life as we know it, throw us off axis, and we lose our center on the One. Satan, Hebrew for "enemy," seeks to distance and isolate us from God. Imagine concentric circles with a bull's-eye in the middle. The farther we are away from the center, the greater the degree of exile we experience. The degree to which we are disconnected or distanced from the center is the degree to which our lives come out of divine alignment into misalignment. Some of the foremost Hebrew terms for sin connect to the concept of being misaligned. *Avon* means "twisted or crooked." The word *sin* in both Hebrew and Greek means "missing the mark or falling short." In other words, it means missing or distanced from the center. The difference between exile and redemption is an issue of proximity. How far are we from the Redeemer, who is our center? Remember the story when the teacher of the law came to Jesus and asked, "Of all the commandments, which is the most important?" (Mark 12:28 NIV). Yeshua responded, "You are not far from the kingdom of God" (Mark 12:34 NIV). Yeshua invites us into proximity—far or near. In Isaiah 57:19, He says, "*Shalom, shalom* to him who is far and to him who is near."

EXILE AND REDEMPTION ARE ONE LETTER APART

Here's another mini Hebrew lesson. In Hebrew, there is a one letter difference between the words for exile and redemption. The word for exile is *Golah*. Now, the first letter of the Hebrew alphabet is *Aleph*. This letter begins most of the names for God.

When you add *Aleph* to the word for exile, the word becomes *Geulah* and means redemption. When we add God into the midst of exile, we end up with redemption.

The Promise of Rededicating . . .

BECOMING CENTERED

Friends, the focus of *Chanukah* is rededicating ourselves to God and recentering our lives close to Him, which results in intimacy and connection. During this season of *Chanukah*, we must take an honest inventory of what is central in our lives. Around what does our world revolve? What causes our lives to spin? Is it our career? Is it our family? Do our possessions own us?

If our lives do not revolve around Messiah Yeshua, then we are being taken for a spin, just like the *dreidel.* If we build our lives on any false axis, it will not spin forever but come tumbling down. Our sincere desire should be to seek God above all else with reckless abandon until He becomes our center again.

"BY MY SPIRIT" YESTERDAY AND TODAY

The primary passage of Scripture for the prophetic reading during *Chanukah*, called the *haftorah*, is Zechariah 4:6: "'Not by might, nor by power, but by my Spirit,' says the LORD Almighty" (NIV).

This same verse is the theme verse for the modern-day State of Israel. In fact, the emblem for the State of Israel has the seven-branched *menorah* embroidered on it.

The seven branches of the *menorah* correspond with the seven Hebrew words of this verse in Zechariah. The national seal for Israel also includes the two olive branches from Zechariah 4 next to the *menorah* that "pour out golden oil through two gold tubes" (v. 12 NLT), symbolizing the miracle of provision for the Maccabees. The modern State of Israel sees itself like the Maccabees, and the secular founders recognize that Israel becoming a nation again was nothing less than a Maccabean-type miracle.

As mentioned in chapter 6, Jewish history defies any odds:

A West Point general once remarked that though the US Military Academy studies wars fought throughout the world, they do not study the Six Day Way—because what concerns West Point is strategy and tactics, not miracles.[5]

The question is, Are we trusting in Him?

LAY IT ALL DOWN

One of my favorite stories of trust involves a couple I knew from the East Coast who desperately wanted to have children but were barren. One day, the messianic congregation to which they belonged called an emergency congregational meeting. There was an amazing opportunity to buy a new property for their gathering place. They were not a wealthy congregation. The staff called the meeting because they were about twenty thousand dollars short of the amount they needed.

---

5 Steven DeNoon, *Israel, Are They Still God's People?* (North Fort Myers, FL: Faithful Life Publishers, 2011), 214.

For years, the infertile couple had painstakingly put away all their savings for fertility treatments, which totaled twenty thousand dollars. At first, they struggled, but then the couple felt God speak to them very clearly. They turned to one another, "I think God wants us to give away the money. We have to understand that if we give away this money, we will never have a child."

Yet, they felt God told them to do this. So they wrote the check, and they gave the gift. They abandoned their dreams and put their trust and faith in God alone. They laid it down on the altar. Just after they gave up their inheritance, they got pregnant. Not once, not twice, but three times—God answered the cry of their hearts.

This story encapsulates the miracle of *Chanukah* to me. It asks this question: Who are you going to trust? Like Abraham, like the Maccabees, like the Messiah Himself, this couple was willing to lay down their dreams and hopes and choose to be utterly dependent on God. As they built God's house, God built theirs. Missionary and martyr Jim Elliot puts it beautifully: "He is no fool who gives what he cannot keep to gain what he cannot lose."[6]

CAPTURING THE LIGHT

In John 10, Jesus is in Jerusalem for the celebration of *Chanukah*. Before that, in John 9, He performs a miracle for the man who has been blind since birth. Right before He spits in the mud and places it on the sightless eyes, He calls Himself

---

6 Elisabeth Elliot, *Shadow of the Almighty* (Peabody, MA: Hendrickson Publishers, Inc., 1958, 1989), 17.

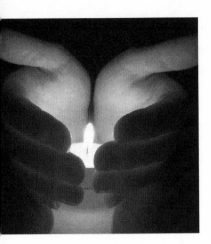

"the light of the world" (v. 5). The light He is referring to in Himself, I believe, is the divine light, which was the very first thing the Lord brought forth at Creation. Since the sun was not created until the third day, rabbis traditionally understood that it was a special celestial light that emanated from God and illuminated all creation. It is the same light that illumines the New Jerusalem in Revelation 21:23: "The city has no need for the sun or the moon to shine on it, for the glory of God lights it."

With the lighting of each *Chanukah* candle, we are rededicating ourselves to and recentering on the Messiah, the divine Light. In fact, in Matthew 5:14, Jesus calls **us**, His followers, "the light of the world." Like the Levites of long ago, we are called to steward that light. We are reminded to *see* the Light of God's promises and *be* the Light of the promises of God. We must extinguish anything that tries to diminish that calling at all costs.

The *great miracle that happened there* is the miracle of *Chanukah* that is for us today as well: even when the oil runs low, God keeps the oil burning. He is not limited by a limited supply or overcome by overwhelming odds. Remember, God says, "Not by might nor by power, but by my Spirit," which is unchanging (Zech. 4:6 NIV).

TRANSFORMATION STARTS WITH YOU

Let this season of *Chanukah* remind us that He is going to complete His work within us.

I am sure of this very thing—that He who began a **good work** in you will carry it on **to completion** until the Day of Messiah *Yeshua*. (Phil. 1:6)

Chanukah and the celebration of the light of the Messiah must remind you that He has hand-chosen you before the world's foundations to embark on a journey into the fullness of your destiny. Yesteryear, God multiplied the oil and delivered the many into the hands of the few. Today, He wants to increase the oil of intimacy in you and make you victors instead of victims. He wants you to be aware of who you are in Him—overcomers like the Maccabees. Are the promises and presence of God fully possessing you? Are you shining brightly like the miracle *menorah* of the Maccabees? Is your life centered around Him so that you are in perfect alignment with His will?

Remember, God must first set our hearts ablaze with radical passion for Yeshua-Jesus. Intimacy is what ignites change, first within us and then in the world. Let a fire for spiritual transformation be lit in you during the *Chanukah* season, and may it begin to burn within you. Remember, like the Messiah, you are the light of the world.

HOW TO CELEBRATE
Chanukah

1. **Get a *hannukiah*.** We light a *menorah* every night to celebrate the miracles of the oil and the war. The essential thing you need to celebrate *Chanukah* is a nine-branched candelabra called a *hannukiah* (or *menorah*, although technically a *menorah* is a seven-branched candelabra) and candles. Eight of the branches symbolize the eight nights the oil lasted, while the ninth one (at a different height, usually higher than the rest) is called the *shamash*, or helper candle, and is used to light the rest of the candles. On the first night, the *shamash* is lit, a blessing is spoken (see prayers below), and the first candle is lit (candles are lit from left to right). On the second night, the *shamash* plus two candles are lit and so on until the eighth night, when all nine branches are burning with lit candles. Traditionally, the lighted *hannukiah* is placed near a window, a public place, to publicize the miracle of *Chanukah*.

2. **Play *dreidel*.** A four-sided top called a *dreidel* or *sivivon* is used to play a gambling game with small candies or

nuts. Players get an equal amount of candies and place some of the candies into a pot in the center. Players take turns spinning the *dreidel*. Each side of the *dreidel* bears a letter that tells the players whether to put in or take out candies. The game ends when someone has all the candies or when the candies have all been eaten (typically in homes with small children.)

3. **Give small tokens to children.** Small gifts of money (*gelt*) are given to children on each night of *Chanukah*. Chocolate coins are also popular as treats and gifts during *Chanukah*. Consider giving each child a $5 blank check each night to make out to the charity of their choice.

4. **Eat the foods cooked in oil.** *Chanukah* wouldn't be the same without the traditional *latkes* and applesauce. *Lat-*

kes (pancakes made from shredded potatoes, onions, *matzoh* meal, and salt) are fried in oil to crispy golden brown, then served with applesauce (and often sour cream). The frying oil recalls the miracle of the oil for those celebrating. Small powdered-sugar donuts called *sufgeniot* are also a popular *Chanukah* treat, especially in Israel. Forget the waistline because fried, oil-rich foods are the theme for this holiday.

5. **Practice *Tikun Olam*.** *Chanukah* offers a wonderful chance to talk with children about what they believe in and the importance of standing up for your beliefs. Find causes that encourage and support free speech and religious freedom, and help them to spread those messages centuries after the miracle of *Chanukah*. Remember, *Chanukah* is the story of the Israelites fighting for their belief in religious freedom.

Chanukah Menorah Prayers

Chanukah Candle Lighting Prayer

The first two blessings below are recited on each of the eight nights of *Chanukah*. The third one is a blessing of joy, which is traditionally recited on each Jewish festival and is recited only the first time the *Chanukah menorah* is lit.

Prayer 1

Barukh atta ADONAI, *Elohenu Melekh ha'olam, asher kideshanu be-mitzvotav vetzivanu le-hadlik ner shel Chanukka.*

Blessed are You, Lord, our God, sovereign of the universe who has sanctified us with His commandments and commanded us to light the lights of *Chanukah*.

Prayer 2

Barukh atta ADONAI, *Elohenu Melekh ha'olam, she'asa nissim la'avotenu, bayyamim hahem bazzeman hazzeh.*

Blessed are You, Lord our God, King of the universe, who wrought miracles for our fathers in days of old, at this season.

Prayer 3

Barukh atta ADONAI, *Elohenu Melekh ha'olam shehecheyanu, vekiyyemanu vehigi'anu lazzeman hazzeh.*

Blessed are You, Lord our God, King of the universe, who has kept us alive and has preserved us and enabled us to reach this time.

Prayer 4

Hanneirot hallalu anachnu madlikin 'al hannissim ve'al han-niflaot 'al hatteshu'ot ve'al hammilchamot she'asita laavoteinu bayyamim haheim, (u)bazzeman hazeh 'al yedei kohanekha hakkedoshim. Vekhol-shemonat yemei Hanukkah hanneirot hallalu kodesh heim, ve-ein lanu reshut lehishtammesh baheim ella lir'otam bilvad kedei lehodot ul'halleil leshimcha haggadol 'al nissekha ve'al nifleotekha ve'al yeshu'otekha.

We light these lights for the miracles and the wonders, for the redemption and the battles that You made for our forefathers, in those days at this season, through Your holy priests. During all eight days of Hanukkah these lights are sacred, and we are not permitted to make ordinary use of them except for to look at them in order to express thanks and praise to Your great name for Your miracles, Your wonders, and Your salvation.

Purim is all about the *invisibility* of God. *Purim* highlights His *hiddenness*. This holiday is all about people coming forth and taking a stance based on their trust and faith in a silent, unseen God.

CHAPTER EIGHT

PURIM

For such a time as this . . .

Esther 4:14

The following words were found scratched into a cellar wall in Cologne, Germany, by a Jewish person hiding from persecution from the Nazis:

> I believe in the sun, even when it is not shining.
> I believe in love, even when not feeling it.
> I believe in God, even when He is silent.[1]

The holiday of *Chanukah* that we've just explored is all about God expressing Himself very visibly through His supernatural provision. He delivered the many into the hands of the few and multiplied one day's ration of oil to keep the *menorah* burning for eight days.

Purim is all about the *invisibility* of God. *Purim* highlights His *hiddenness*. This holiday is all about people coming forth and taking a stance based on their trust and faith in a silent, unseen God. To understand this, you have to know how the holiday came to be.

Let's say that the ancient Persians knew how to party. The backstory to *Purim* began with a party—a six-month drinking and feasting fest given by King Xerxes, also known as King Ahasuerus, of the Persian Empire. This 180-day celebration was for more than 100 of the provinces in his vast kingdom.

At the end of this multi-month mania, King Xerxes called for a seven-day drinking party for all of Shushan residents, both for the rich and the poor. I can feel a hangover just thinking about it.

---

1 Anthony Scioli and Henry Biller, *Hope in the Age of Anxiety* (New York: Oxford University Press, 2009), 22.

When they finished that festivity, the women, led by Queen Vashti, held a separate seven-day party in the royal court. Xerxes got a little drunk and commanded his queen to appear before him and parade her beauty before all the people, old and young, rich and poor, Jew and Gentile. Vashti refused. An indignant Xerxes was counseled to control her rebellion by dethroning her. The party was over for Vashti, as well as the other residents of Shushan. A beauty contest was now underway, designed to search for Vashti's replacement from among the empire's most eligible young ladies. The saddened Xerxes desired a new queen. It was the ancient world's version of *The Bachelor*.

THE JEWISH QUEEN OF THE GENTILE EMPIRE

Esther was orphaned in her youth and raised by her cousin Mordecai, who held some position within the royal court. They were Jews from the tribe of Benjamin whose people fell into captivity during the Babylonian exile, followed by the Persian exile. It was not widely known that Mordecai and Esther were related by blood, so she was eligible to participate in the parade of Persian beauties before the king. Mordecai forbade her to tell anyone that she was Jewish. Out of all the fair faces in Xerxes' kingdom, Esther found favor with the king, and he chose her to be his queen. Little did Xerxes know he crowned a Jew to be the queen of his pagan people.

CHANCE BY DESIGN

I'm going to interrupt the story here to bring attention to God's perfect sense of irony. The word *Pur* means a single "lot." *Purim* is the plural form of the word *Pur* and means "lots." The practice of casting lots is mentioned seventy times in the Old Testament and seven times in the New Testament. The casting of lots is all about chance. The closest modern practice to casting lots is likely flipping a coin. Therefore, this holiday is named after a game of chance. However, it is chance by *divine design*, which you will see as the story continues.

SAVE THE KING!

Going about his court business one day, Mordecai overheard a plot to kill the king. He informed Esther, now the queen, and together they foiled the evil plans. Mordecai's name went down in the annals of the king as the one who helped save Xerxes. Second-in-command to Xerxes was a man named Haman, who was a descendant of the king of the Amalekites, a nomadic people who harassed and attacked the Hebrew people during their exodus from Egypt. They were so wicked that God commanded King Saul, "Go, attack the Amalekites and totally destroy all that belongs to them. Do not spare them; put to death men and women, children and infants, cattle and sheep, camels and donkeys" (1 Sam. 15:3 NIV). Saul did not fully obey God's command and allowed some of these evil ones to live. Haman descended from those who were left.

Hubris filled Haman, and he believed that everyone should bow down to him. Because Haman was such a *rasha*, a wicked man, everyone submitted out of fear. Except for Mordecai. Haman, according to Jewish tradition, wore a large idol around his neck. That was a big no-no in Jewish thought. A good Jewish boy like

Mordy would not bow to an idol or even give the appearance of bowing to an idol like the one that hung from Haman's neck. Just like his Jewish brothers before him—Shadrach, Meshach, and Abednego—Mordecai would never bow. Mordecai's apparent lack of respect infuriated Haman. And Haman's wrath only intensified when he found out Mordecai was Jewish. I can hear the cranks turning in Haman's head: *He is not going to bow down to me. His people probably will not bow down to me. So it is not just enough for me to get rid of him. I am going to wipe out all the Jews in Shushan. Everyone who is of Mordecai's tribe must die!*

Let's stop for a moment and examine this situation. Because Saul disobeyed God, Haman lived and threatened yet another lethal attack on the Jews. The instruction God gave in 1 Samuel 15:3 seemed out of character for God—a merciful Creator giving merciless orders. Kill everyone and everything! But He sees the beginning from the end. He knew that if one seed were left, the threat would grow again. Indeed, it did.

With a fiendishness of fairy-tale caliber, Haman plotted the demise of Mordecai and his people. He counseled the king:

> "There is a certain people dispersed among the peoples in all the provinces of your kingdom who keep themselves separate. Their customs are different from those of all other people, and they do not obey the king's laws; it is not in the king's best interest to tolerate them. If it pleases the king, let a decree be issued to destroy them, and I will give ten thousand talents of silver to the king's administrators for the royal treasury." (Est. 3:8–9 NIV)

The king answered, "Go ahead; it's your money—do whatever you want with those people." Mordecai was sold for silver. Ring a bell? Little did Xerxes know that he just endorsed his queen's execution.

WHY DID HAMAN CHANCE IT?

Haman was left smacking his lips in delight with the genocidal question: *On which day should the Jews die?* He decided that the game of chance known as casting lots would determine the fate of Mordecai's (and Esther's) people. Chance is the ultimate insult to purposeful design or intentionality. By casting lots, Haman was thumbing his nose at God and God's people. Like his ancestor Amalek, who didn't pay attention to the stories of the disasters that plagued Egypt before the Exodus, Haman had the *chutzpah* to think that he could decide the fate of God's people based on how the chips fell—or, in this case, the lots. According to Esther 3:7–13, the lots landed on the thirteenth day of the twelfth month of Adar. Fate would be sealed that day. But whose fate?

LOTS AND PLOTS

Mordecai learned of this new plot, this time to kill him and his people. He couldn't go to the king because he knew that Haman had sway with him. He had to get word to the queen, whom Xerxes (Ahasuerus) had no idea was a Jew. When he sent word to Esther, she was hesitant. You have to understand that she couldn't simply walk up to her husband and say, "Honey, I need to talk to you." To go uninvited before the king could mean execution. However, to not go was *certain* death for her and her people. Even so, Mordecai had to persuade her.

> "For if you remain silent at this time, relief and deliverance for the Jews will arise from another place, but you and your father's family will perish. And who knows but that you have come to your royal position for such a time as this?" (Est. 4:14 NIV)

For such a time as this. These words have been echoed over the centuries to address all sorts of situations. Why? They carry such weight of truth. Esther was not there by chance. Esther was there by design to save her people. Now, the question was, would she?

Esther told Mordecai to tell the Jews of Shushan to fast for her (Est. 4:16). Esther then prayed and fasted with all the Jews of Shushan for three days, knowing that seeking an audience with the king was "not according to the law" (Est. 4:16). She resolutely said, "So if I perish, I perish!" (Est. 4:16). After the three days of fasting, she approached the king. When the king saw her coming, he extended his scepter to her as a sign of acceptance. "What is it, Queen Esther? What is your request? Even up to half the kingdom, it will be given to you" (5:3 NIV). Her request was simple. She wanted a meal with him and Haman, at which time she would make known her desire. "'Bring Haman at once,' the king said, 'so that we may do what Esther asks'" (v. 5 NIV).

Notice that Xerxes wanted to please her immediately. Her favor with the king was evident. They feasted, and the king asked of Esther her request. She petitioned for another banquet with the two of them the next evening, promising that she would make her petition known then. Haman was beside himself with happiness, boasting to his friends and family that the only invited guests to the dinner parties with the queen were he and Xerxes—two nights in a row. However, Haman's glee didn't deter him from continuing with his heinous plan for Mordecai's demise. He ordered the building of gallows from which he intended to hang Mordecai on the same day as the second banquet with Xerxes and Esther.

Esther 6 records that insomnia plagued Xerxes on the night before the second dinner. To soothe himself, he ordered the reading of stories from the official record of his reign. To what story do you think the servant opened the journals? It was the record of how Mordecai learned of the plot to kill the king and saved Xerxes' life! Chance? Not by a long shot. "'What honor and recognition has Mordecai received for this?' the king asked. 'Nothing has been done for him,' his attendants answered" (v. 3 NIV). The next day, the king asked for Haman's suggestion for honoring a man who delighted the king. Thinking Xerxes was speaking of him, Haman detailed all that he would like done for him—royal robes, a royal crest on his head, a parade through town on a royal horse. "'Go at once,' the king commanded Haman. 'Get the robe and the horse and do just as you have suggested for Mordecai the Jew, who sits at the king's gate. Do not neglect anything you have recommended'" (v. 10 NIV). Now, friends, I would have loved to have been a fly on the wall in that royal room. Can you imagine Haman's shock at the name of Mordecai? I'm sure Haman was "mord-ified." I love God's sense of humor here. The whole host of heaven's angels must have been rolling with laughter down the celestial streets of gold as Haman paraded Mordecai down the streets of Shushan. Good one, God.

FOR SUCH A TIME AS THIS . . .

Shortly after the parade, the king's servants whisked Haman away to attend the queen's banquet. As the wine and food flowed, the king again asked the desire of his queen. Esther finally answered,

> "If I have found favor with you, Your Majesty, and if it pleases you, **grant me my life—this is my petition. And spare my people—this is my request.** For I and my people have been sold to be destroyed, killed and annihilated." (Est. 7:3–4 NIV)

There. Esther said it. She came clean and stood up for herself and her people. Outraged at this villainous plot, the king demanded the name of the culprit. Esther said, "An adversary and enemy! This vile Haman!" (v. 6 NIV). Haman threw himself on the queen, begging for his life. This molestation of the queen infuriated the king even more. Haman met the end that he had devised for Mordecai. Xerxes ordered Haman's hanging from the very gallows meant for Mordecai.

Esther realized that though Haman's evil plotting was finished, his evil doings were still underway. In Persia, once a decree was ordered, it could not be recanted. She implored the king to issue a counter-decree to Haman's genocidal plan. In short, the Jewish people could defend themselves if attacked. On the thirteenth of Adar, five hundred people in Shushan, including Haman's ten sons, attacked the Jewish people, and all the attackers perished. Throughout the Persian Empire, seventy-five thousand of the Jews' enemies were killed (Est. 9:16). On the fourteenth day of Adar, another three hundred were killed at Shushan.

Mordecai assumed Haman's position as the second most powerful man in Persia. He instituted *Purim*, the Jewish holiday named to honor the sweet irony of God's divine plot behind Haman's haphazard game of lots.

SILENT YET SOVEREIGN

It's interesting to note that the book of Esther was almost excluded from the Bible. The reason for this near miss is that God's name is not mentioned once in the book. How can a book that never mentions God be used in the Bible? But that is precisely the point—the purpose of the book is for God NOT to be mentioned. The story of Esther is all about a veiled God. God does not hide not to be found. God hides because He wants us to go deeper in our relationship with Him and our faith. He seeks to be sought.

I'm reminded of a story of a notable rabbi who had a grandson. One day his grandson was playing hide-and-seek with another boy. His grandson remained in his hiding place for a long time, assuming that his friend would try and find him. Finally, he left his hiding place and saw that his friend was gone. The boy started to cry, and he ran to his grandfather. The rabbi began to cry. The grandson turned to his grandfather and said, "Why are *you* crying?" The rabbi said, "God too says: 'I hide, but there is no one to look for me.'"[2] Like the boy's friend, will we walk away or keeping looking until He is found?

UNSEEN BEHIND THE SCENES

Bobby, a director friend of mine, directed a compelling film about a father's sacrificial love for his son. Bobby never appears once in the movie, but if you know him, you'll notice his fingerprints are all over this modern-day parable. It is the same with God in the book of Esther. God is never seen or mentioned, but He is orchestrating the events in the story, calling the shots behind the lens, so to speak, like an adept director.

Let's revisit specific plot points to magnify His divine fingerprints:

- A good Jewish girl, Esther, becomes queen of the Gentile superpower of the day.
- Her cousin Mordecai overhears a plot to kill the king and saves his life, which gets recorded in the chronicles of the king.
- An enemy of the Jews, Haman, who is the right-hand man to the king, plots to kill Mordecai and all the Jews in the empire's provinces.
- One night King Xerxes, known in Hebrew as Ahasuerus, can't sleep, so an assistant reads from the

---

2 Abraham Joshua Heschel, *Man Is Not Alone: A Philosophy of Religion* (New York: Farrar, Straus and Giroux, 1976), 154.

royal records to quell his insomnia and happens to choose the story of Mordecai's foiling the murderous plot to kill him.

- Xerxes asks Haman to honor Mordecai in a royal procession through town.
- Mordecai urges Esther to take a stand against Haman and let his heinous plan against the Jews, *her* people, be known to the king.
- Esther finds faith enough to risk death to save her people and informs the king of Haman's wicked wile.
- Haman dies by the method he designed for Mordecai.
- All the enemies of the Jews who attack them while carrying out Haman's plan are killed themselves, totaling in the tens of thousands.
- Xerxes bestows Haman's royal title upon Mordecai, and Haman's fortune is divided between Mordecai and Esther.

It is a tightly written script and divinely directed by the unseen God at work behind the scenes.

DOUBT AS A DOOR

I learned the following truth from a college professor who spoke these words of utmost faith during a time of utter tragedy: *When you cannot see the hand of God, you have to trust the heart of God.* I want to focus on the word *trust*. When we can't see God, we have to trust He is still there looking out for us and working all things for the good of those who belong to Him (Rom. 8:28). I liken God to oxygen—we can't see it, but it is there, or we're not breathing.

Trust is the deadbolt on the door that keeps the enemy out. Without the lock, the door of doubt opens us up to the attack of the evil one. Haman was a descendant of Agag, who was a descendant of Amalek, the leader of the Amalekites, the tribe of people who attacked the Hebrew people upon their exodus from Egypt. In Jewish thought, Haman and Amalek are not just historical persons but also the spirits of evil, degradation, doubt, and destruction. These spirits prey upon the weak and vulnerable in every season and every generation. The name of Amalek in Hebrew has a numerical value of 240, which is the same numerical value as the Hebrew word for doubt, *safek*. Doubt is insidious and sly. It snakes its way into us without our being aware. How does doubt operate?

Doubt makes us question. We question ourselves and question God. Let's go back to the beginning in the garden. The serpent tempted Eve in the form of a question: "Did God really say . . . ?" (Gen. 3:3). The evil one makes us question our spiritual identity, God's promises, even the existence of God altogether. Why did Esther hesitate to go before Xerxes? True, it was protocol that the king had to request one's presence with him—so Esther risked death in entering his presence. However, if she didn't *doubt* his affection for her and her favor with him, she wouldn't have had to work up the courage to seek his audience. *Courage* is the next focus word.

COURAGE DOES NOT COMPROMISE

Noted author C. S. Lewis wrote, "Courage is not simply just one of the virtues, but the form of every virtue at the testing point."[3]

Mordecai was the epitome of courage. He took a stand against Haman, the prime minister to the king. He courageously said, "I am a Jew, unwilling to bow before anyone or anything." His actions reflect how Nelson Mandela described courage: "Courage is not the absence of fear but the triumph over it."[4]

In messianic Jewish thought, Mordecai can be seen as a type of Yeshua. Yeshua would not bow down to the king of this world and give in to temptation. Mordecai and Yeshua were both falsely accused. Lots were cast in both their cases. Both were sentenced to death on a tree, one on a pole and another on the cross. Both had royal garments put upon them and paraded through the streets. Both had betrayers, and Judas himself met death on a tree just like Haman.

Courage does not compromise. Courage dispels doubt, just like Mordecai talked Esther out of doubt into her destiny.

THE GOD OF CHANCE

A significant element to this story is that Mordecai and Esther reversed the result of King Saul's compromise when he disobeyed God and didn't wipe out all the Amalekites from which Haman descended.

---

3 C. S. Lewis, *A Year with C. S. Lewis: Daily Readings from His Classic Works* (New York: Harper Collins, 2003), 343.

4 Nelson R. Mandela, *Notes to the Future: Words of Wisdom* (New York: Simon & Schuster, Inc., 2012), 18.

Here's the connection: King Saul was from the tribe of Benjamin. Mordecai and Esther were also from the tribe of Benjamin. Through Mordecai and Esther, God allowed the tribe of Benjamin to prevail where Saul failed centuries before. God is so gracious and compassionate that He delights in extending grace. God does not fail or abandon us but often allows us to repeatedly take the test until we pass it. Finally, the tribe got it right. In a way, God is a God of chance—second chances.

FROM DOUBT TO DESTINY

When Esther transitioned from doubt to destiny, courage was the bridge she had to walk upon to get to the other side. Once there, she found joy—the joy of realizing the king's favor upon her, the joy of saving herself and her people, the joy of seeing Mordecai replace Haman, the joy of receiving the spoils from Haman's estate. Every one of us has a *for such a time as this* moment when our destiny is within reach. We can decide if we are going to walk into it or walk away from it. Each of us is designed for our God-ordained purpose, and if we say yes to His plan, there is joy.

WINNIE THE POOH AND *PURIM*

Purim is a time of great *simcha*—great joy, grand celebration. It is one of the happiest seasons of the entire Jewish year. As it states in Esther 9:22, *Purim* looks back on "the month when their sorrow was turned into joy." Joy is to abound during this holiday. *Purim* is a season when God wants to turn our sadness into gladness, our darkness to light, our heaviness to lightness, our destruction to salvation, our Eeyore into Tigger—*what?*

When my sons were very young, their favorite cartoon was *Winnie the Pooh*. I observed the characters quite often and discovered what I call the Eeyore Syndrome. "Good morning, Pooh Bear," says a gloomy Eeyore. "If it is a good morning . . . Which I doubt."[5] The Eeyore Syndrome is typically sadness. Some people are so depressed, they do not even have moments of happiness. It is a hopeless, faithless, anxious, emotional pattern of sadness called depression. Sadness is rooted in the spirit of Amalek and has to be rooted out. In Jewish thought, depression is one of the most dangerous and destructive forces to our spiritual life. It is a curse that cripples us and robs us of our ability to love and serve God and others. In some ways, depression is a defense mechanism. If we don't get too excited about anything, we can't be disappointed. We numb ourselves. In doing so, we numb our pain but also our ability to feel joy.

I watched a YouTube clip from *The Onion* that was a parody of a pharmaceutical commercial and a report on it. It was basically about how happy people are destroying the world. The pharmaceutical reps interview a woman who says, in effect, "I didn't realize my happiness was a sickness, and my cheerfulness was ruining my relationships with people. Then I took this depressing pill, and it made me better."[6] We live in a society that is so depressed that we think it is normal.

---

5 A. A. Milne, *Winnie-the-Pooh* (New York: Dutton Children's Books, 2009), 72.

6 "FDA Approves Depressant Drug for the Annoyingly Cheerful," *The Onion*, February 12, 2009, https://www.youtube.com/watch?v=jd4tugPM83c.

Joy is completely counter to depression. Joy is an abiding sense of *wonderful* that is beyond happiness; it is an optimistic sunshine-filled emotional pattern that we can refer to as the Tigger Syndrome. Tigger is always joyous, no matter what is happening. He reflects pure, biblical joy, which is not rooted in situations and circumstances. Real biblical joy has no connection to happiness, which is shallower than joy. The root word *happy* comes from the word *happenstance*, which is based on circumstance. Happiness is from the outside in. Joy is transcendent. Joy is from the inside out.

So many days when my boys were young, I came home exhausted and walked through the front door only to be greeted by pure joy in the form of my two boys. "Daddy! Daddy!" They jumped on me and hugged me, and my exhaustion shifted into exhilaration. Joy is contagious. As our sages say, "*Simcha poretz geder*"—joy breaks all barriers. Joy empowers us; it gives us encouragement, zeal, enthusiasm, optimism, and it allows us to transcend all obstacles—even the fear of death itself.

I love the word *poretz*[7] because, in Jewish thought, it is one of the names of the Messiah. "One breaking through [*poretz*, meaning Messiah] will go up before them. They will break through, pass through the gate and go out by it" (Mic. 2:13). It should be no surprise that the Messiah is the descendant of Perez (*Peretz*) from the tribe of Judah. Peretz means "the one who breaks forth from his mother's womb." Joy is the key to breaking the evil one's yoke and receiving a greater anointing in our lives. Depression

---

7 You can learn more about *poretz* and the decade of breakthrough in my book *Breakthrough: Living a Life That Overflows*. It's available at Amazon.

robs us of our ability to serve God and others, but joy loosens us and sets us free to be whom God intended us to be.

The Bible tells us that when Joseph was thrown into the pit and his brothers told his father, Jacob, that his beloved Joseph was dead, depression came upon Jacob and the spirit of *nevuah*, the spirit of prophecy, left him. On the day they were reunited, such joy broke forth in Jacob's heart that the Spirit of God returned. In Genesis 49, he gathers his sons and says, "Gather together so that I can tell you what will happen to you in the last days" (v. 1). He prophesies over each of them.

Joy is the second fruit of the Spirit in Galatians 5:22–23. I believe joy is childlike, and Jesus gives us one of the reasons in Luke 18:16: "For the kingdom of God belongs to such as these [the children]." In Yeshua's final prayer in John 17, He prays, "I say these words while I am still in the world, so that they may have the My joy made full in themselves" (v. 13). God wants us to turn the Eeyore-like "oys" into the Tigger-like "joys."

This season of *Purim* is to be a time when joy increases. My Fusion Global ministry celebrates *Purim* by sponsoring Esther's Ball, where we dress up, feast, and party like kings and queens. We interactively tell the story of Esther and ask God to remove every obstacle and barrier to our joy, just like He removed Haman, just like He removed the doors that separated Esther from the king. Just like the curtain was torn from top to bottom when Yeshua was crucified, no longer separating the people from the Holy of Holies. Joy is transformative. For Esther, faith overcame fear and moved her into her destiny, where she found joy. Joy awaits us. We were designed for it, and God wants nothing less for us.

A COMMON DESTINY

Pure and undefiled religion before our God and Father is
this: to care for orphans and widows in their distress.
James 1:27

A cartoon often portrays joy in the form of a bouncing tiger or a flitting butterfly over a field of flowers. In reality, joy is the three-letter word for *power* on all levels—emotional and spiritual, which translates into physical. Nehemiah 8:10 tells us, "For **the joy of ADONAI** is your strength." When we have the joy of the Lord, our priorities shift.

When we put Yeshua-Jesus first, then we will naturally make helping others a priority. Yeshua said that He came to set the captives free.

> The Spirit of the Lord is on me, because he has anointed me to proclaim good news to the poor. He has sent me to proclaim **freedom** for the prisoners . . . to set the oppressed free. (Luke 4:18 NIV)

All of us, indeed, have unique destinies as followers of the Messiah. We also have a common destiny. We are to fight the injustices of our world like Esther and Mordecai had to fight the injustice of Haman's murderous plot. Today, the spirits of Haman and Amalek still prey on the vulnerable and accessible: the sick, the impoverished, the lonely, the desperate.

In a stand against injustice, Fusion Global has cohosted events like the Ball for Justice to raise funds to aid in the rescue of women and children from the merciless, rampant sex trafficking industry. Evil is no respecter of persons; everyone is equal prey.

Like Esther, we have to step out into action and put feet on our faith. Mordecai taught, inspired, and encouraged her, but Esther risked her life to go before the king. It was Esther who risked death so that her people might live. For this reason, this book in the Bible is named after her.

At some point, we all have to choose whether we are going to "go before the king" and move into our destiny or hide in the shadows of the safe zone. The *for such a time as this* verse from Esther 4:14 continues with Mordecai plainly stating, "If you keep quiet at a time like this, deliverance and relief for the Jews will arise from some other place" (NLT).

In other words, someone else will make the difference God has called you to make. God has plans. If we say no to His purposes for our lives, He will find someone who will say yes. If we say yes, then there is alignment with His will. Then, there is joy.

HOW TO CELEBRATE
Purim

1. **Listen to the *Megillah*.** To relive and capture the miraculous events of Purim, **listen to the reading of the *Megillah* (the Scroll of Esther)** twice: once on *Purim* Eve, and again on *Purim* Day. To properly fulfill the *mitzvah* (commandment), it is imperative to hear every word of the *Megillah*. At specific points in the reading, when Haman's name is mentioned, it is customary to twirl *graggers* (*Purim* noisemakers). We use noisemakers to blot out the name of the Amalekite (Haman's people), as instructed in the *Torah* in Exodus 17:14 and Deuteronomy 25:17–19. We are also to stamp our feet to eradicate his evil name. Instruct the children that *Purim* is the only time when it's a *mitzvah* to make noise.

2. **Give to the needy (*Matanot LaEvyonim*).** Awareness and concern for the needy is a year-round responsibility. But on *Purim*, it is a special *mitzvah* to remember the poor.

Give *tsedaka* (charity) to at least two (but preferably more) needy individuals on *Purim* Day. Giving directly to the needy best fulfills the *mitzvah*. However, if you cannot find people in need, place at least two coins into a charity box. As with *Purim*'s other practical aspects, even the very young should be taught to fulfill this *mitzvah*.

3. **Send food portions to friends (*Mishloach Manot*).** On *Purim*, we focus on the importance of unity and friendship by sending gifts of food to friends. **On *Purim* Day, send a gift of at least two kinds of ready-to-eat foods (e.g., pastry, fruit, beverage) to at least one favored friend.** A third party should deliver the gifts. In addition to sending their special gifts of food to their friends, children make excited messengers for gifts to others.

4. **Eat, drink, and be merry.** *Purim* is celebrated with **a special festive feast on *Purim* Day**, at which family and friends gather together to rejoice in the *Purim* spirit. It is traditional to drink wine.

Special Prayers (*Al HaNissim, Torah* reading)

On *Purim*, we include the *Al HaNissim* prayer, which retells the *Purim* miracle, in the evening, morning and afternoon prayers, as well as in the grace after meals. In the morning service, there is a **special reading from the *Torah* scroll** in the synagogue (Ex. 17:8–16).

Purim Customs: Masquerades and *Hamantashen*

A time-honored *Purim* custom is for **children as well as adults** to **dress up** and **disguise themselves behind masks**—an allusion to the fact that the miracle of *Purim* was disguised in natural garments.[8] This custom symbolizes that God was hidden in the book of Esther until the end. This is also the significance behind a traditional *Purim* food, the *hamantashen*—a pastry whose filling is hidden within a three-cornered crust.

---

8 "Because of a series of incredible circumstances that led to the Jews prevailing, it is believed that God himself performed the miracle of Purim though disguised in natural garments. . . . Rabbi Shmuel Schlanger [said,] . . . 'Purim is based on a day of concealment so we can remember that God may very well be concealed among us, working His miracles.'" Teresa Adamo, "Making Lots of Noise on Purim," Chabad of Bakersfield, March 21, 2003, https://www.chabadofbakersfield.com/templates/articlecco_cdo/aid/74669/jewish/Purim.htm.

JEWISH HOLIDAYS 2020–2030

YEAR	PURIM	PASSOVER	SHAVUOT/ PENTECOST	ROSH HASHANAH	YOM KIPPUR	SUKKOT	CHANUKAH
2020	March 10	April 9	May 29	Sept. 19	Sept. 28	Oct. 3	Dec. 11
2021	Feb. 26	March 28	May 17	Sept. 7	Sept. 16	Sept. 21	Nov. 29
2022	March 17	April 16	June 5	Sept. 26	Oct. 5	Oct. 10	Dec. 19
2023	March 7	April 6	May 26	Sept. 16	Sept. 25	Sept. 30	Dec. 8
2024	March 24	April 23	June 12	Oct. 3	Oct. 12	Oct. 17	Dec. 26
2025	March 14	April 13	June 2	Sept. 23	Oct. 2	Oct.7	Dec. 15
2026	March 3	April 2	May 22	Sept. 12	Sept. 21	Sept. 26	Dec. 5
2027	March 23	April 22	June 11	Oct. 2	Oct. 11	Oct. 16	Dec. 25
2028	March 12	April 11	May 31	Sept. 21	Sept. 30	Oct. 5	Dec. 13
2029	March 1	March 31	May 20	Sept. 10	Sept. 19	Sept. 24	Dec. 2
2030	March 19	April 18	June 7	Sept. 28	Oct. 7	Oct. 12	Dec. 21

The Jewish holidays move in the Western (or Gregorian) calendar because the traditional Jewish calendar is a lunar calendar. All Jewish holidays begin eighteen minutes before sunset the evening **before** the date specified on the calendar.

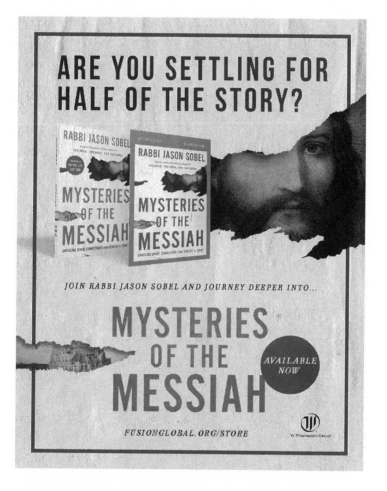

JOURNEY WITH ME,
RABBI JASON SOBEL
TO THE HOLY LAND,
ISRAEL
VISIT:
ROCKROADRABBITOURS.COM
fusionglobal.org
@rabbijasonsobel

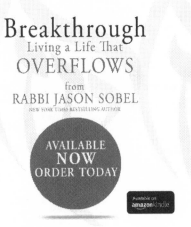